Bloody Jack

Bloody Jack

THE UNIVERSITY OF ALBERTA PRESS

Dennis Cooley

Published by
The University of Alberta Press
Ring House 2
Edmonton, Alberta T6G 2E1

Copyright © Dennis Cooley 2002

NATIONAL LIBRARY OF CANADA CATALOGUING IN PUBLICATION DATA

Cooley, Dennis, 1944–
    Bloody Jack / Dennis Cooley. — Rev. ed.

    Poems.
    ISBN 0-88864-391-8

    1. Krafchenko, Jack—Poetry. I. Title.
PS8555.O575B6 2002   C811'.54   C2002-911375-X
PR9199.3.C642B57 2002

All rights reserved. No part of this publication may be produced, stored in a retrieval system, or transmitted in any forms or by any means, electronic, mechanical, photocopying, recording, or otherwise, without the prior written consent of the copyright owner or a licence from The Canadian Copyright Licensing Agency (Access Copyright). For an Access Copyright license, visit www.accesscopyright.ca or call toll free: 1-800-893-5777.

A volume in (cuRRents), a Canadian literature series. Jonathan Hart, series editor.
Book design by Alan Brownoff.
Publication assistance by Leslie Vermeer.
Printed and bound in Canada by Houghton-Boston, Saskatoon, Saskatchewan.
∞Printed on acid-free paper.

The University of Alberta Press is committed to protecting our natural environment. As part of our efforts, this book is printed on stock produced by New Leaf Paper: it contains 100% post-consumer recycled fibres and is acid- and chlorine-free.

The University of Alberta Press acknowledges the financial support of the Government of Canada through the Book Publishing Industry Development Program for its publishing activities. The Press also gratefully acknowledges the support received for its program from the Canada Council for the Arts.

with thanks to:
Slawko Klymkiw, Wayne Tefs, Diane Cooley, David Arnason, David Carr, Megan Cooley, Robert Kroetsch, Ken Hughes, Jordan Ritchey, Lawrence Ritchey, Patricia Sanders, Jim Donoghue, Karen Clavelle, Leslie Vermeer and, especially, Dana Cooley.

                so help me
          they did
                        help me so
  much i appreciate
                what
       they did

acknowledgements:
Some of these poems have appeared, sometimes in slightly different form, in the following magazines: *Dandelion, Arts Manitoba, CVII, Camrose Review, Rampike, Prairie Fire, NeWest Review, Fiddlehead, Canadian Forum* and *Ariel*, and in the book *Sunfall*. The musical settings for "birds of a feather," "the end of the line," and "by the red" are composed by Lawrence Ritchey and are reproduced with his permission. The first edition of *Bloody Jack* was published by Turnstone Press in 1984.

sources:
I have taken and often modified material from several sources: *The Manitoba Free Press*; Ben Rolph's book John Krafchenko, The Canadian Outlaw; Sylvanus Stall, *What A Young Husband Ought to Know* and *What A Young Man Ought to Know*; Corporal Robert Hutchison, *A Century of Service: A History of the Winnipeg Police Force 1874–1974*; Rev. Wellington Bridgman, *Breaking Prairie Sod*; F. Dojacek, *New Ukrainian–English Interpreter*; and John Gray, *The Boy from Winnipeg*.

Introduction

Celebration! That's what all of Dennis Cooley's poetry is finally about. And in this, his blockbuster of a cornucopian text, the celebration is wide ranging and wild. Bloody Jack comes out swinging and dances Ali-like all over the page, stage of its continually unlikely battles with conformity—of life, of law, of genre. Butterfly or bee, stinging or singing, it lets readers assume nothing as it places them in a position of always having to adjust to new moves, odd arrangements, a stubborn refusal, on the part of text and character alike, to stick to the given story. To hell with the story, Bloody Jack says; have a drink, I've something to tell you, a joke, a whispered bit of gossip, a tongue in your ear, or elsewhere.

History/Documentary
History in the text: There was a historical John Krafchenko, a "Canadian Outlaw," deserving of at least one popular biography, but Cooley is not really interested in re-telling his story in a series of poems. Although Bloody Jack offers its readers something that might remind them of many other Canadian documentary poems, in fact it undermines the documentary impulse at every turn. In doing so, it shows itself as much closer to Ondaatje's The Collected Works of Billy the Kid than, say, Gutteridge's Tecumseh. Cooley, as his study of the former suggests, shares with Ondaatje an interest in using documents in order to subvert the apparently solid reality they represent, and does so in Bloody Jack with an almost terrifying energy and savage delight. This book definitely means to entertain, but it also seeks to keep its audience off balance.

History of the text: Even before the first publication, Bloody Jack had taken on almost mythic, certainly legendary dimensions. Apparently, Cooley has told that story many times:

> I remember when I was doing it, Arnason and Kroetsch were—Kroetsch especially—after me to make it more narrative. I'd show them things along the way, and Kroetsch would say, "Tell the story! What's the story of this guy?" When Arnason assembled the pieces shortly before publication, he grabbed most of the narrative things

and stuck them in. On the sly, I took out some of those and re-inserted some love poems. And a lot of the metalingual pieces got lost, I probably had about twenty pages. Looking back, I wish a few more of them had got in.

I like being able to make those multiple and brief entries, really mobile entries.

Referring to Cooley's "gleeful acts of sabotage" upon the massive manuscript given into Arnason's editorial hands, Mark Liben throws up his hands:

> I recall this barroom tale whenever I attempt to talk about *Bloody Jack*. When I try to offer a reading of this text, to say something coherent about the poetry, I remember Cooley's account of the conflicting battles to reduce the stack of paper into the book I have on the desk beside me now. I remind myself that this book is a by-product of willful and eccentric individuals ... I remind myself that, from first to last, *Bloody Jack* has remained fragmentary and contingent. This is a text that has never been complete, has always been surrounded by lost loose pages.

As Robert Kroetsch once wrote of the first edition, "we quickly discover we do not in fact have a reliable or complete text of the poem." This new edition also remains "fragmentary and contingent," this time upon the new editorial work and play of Cooley the re-visionary and the editors at the University of Alberta Press. More lost loose pages, more new ones. A different text, a still (un)familiar story hidden among the fragments. But some of the play is now directed toward the new edition itself, and its readers, whether or not they know the old one. That is, of course, part of its excessive pleasure.

Scholarship

Works like *Bloody Jack* actually require a kind of scholarship on the part of their writers, and therefore their readers. Of course, in this instance, scholarship is both delivered and derided. Cooley obviously read widely in Manitoba and Winnipeg history, and also brings to bear his long study of literature, which allows him to signal readers the kind of reading experience they are about to enter: Menippean discourse is by its nature fantastic, a wild mix of literary kinds, a satiric attack on what society considers good, virtuous, solid. The language must slide beyond the bounds of propriety, and here it does. All of which necessarily follows upon the epigraph from Julia Kristeva. But an additional epigraph from Barthes alerts readers further to their importance as the destination of "all the quotations that make up a writing," and thus to the need to read this collection of fragments as quotation, and as a construction about which each reader will have the final say. Or should.

Part of the satire is directed against traditional notions of scholarship, and *Bloody Jack* is pleased to attack such conventional thinking in both the imagined critics of the text, and in the figure of "Cooley," the authoritative author himself. Thus the "review" of the book contained within it, the letters to the editor, the interview with a criminal psychologist, who seems all too willing to leap off the high horse of his jargon to tell us that Krafchenko is "certifiably insane." Indeed, although this man begins with what seems to be a careful analysis, it quickly devolves into a series of further wild anecdotes, the tall tales everyone likes to tell, but psychologists should beware.

Parody

Of everything, if only because everything is quotation. Certainly, nothing is sacred in *Bloody Jack*. So it plays games with every genre it touches, sometimes just for laughs, sometimes in order to renew their power. The epic list becomes a cunning linguist's tricks of the trade. Certainly, the text is able simply to take on some forms of rhetoric and by juxtaposition make them self-parodies, at least to contemporary readers enjoying the casual comedic vision of life entertained by *Bloody Jack*.

All the journalistic genres, from the letter to the editor through the review to the editorial, and now including the film script, are placed in a certain parodic jeopardy here, as are such high genres as the lyric, the epic, and, in its different context, the address to the jury. Yet, in some cases, as with the imagist lyric or the apostrophe to the muse, the poems defy the very parody they display to assume a lovely purity. Never on its own, and always surrounded by the laughter of carnivalesque reverses, but somehow or other even the lack of seriousness sometimes falters and a small poem of rare beauty is allowed its place.

Paradox
At the heart of poetry and prayer. In the heart of Krafchenko, and Cooley, as they weave their way through the labyrinth of document, memory, and desire. Built in: to the language, in all its variety, the text plays upon.

Vernacular
Cooley's the one who's said it all about this, but his arguments help to explain what you are about to read:

> assumptions commonly at work: what is a poem? or more immediately, and more usually: what is a good poem? the limits arise for most of us, I think, out of a belief that a poet must "control" "his" material, that the material must be rendered in striking images and arresting metaphors, that the poem must be laden with elegant phrasings and high allusions, that the text must be susceptible to multiple readings (i.e., "for all time"), that the poet must deal with "serious" issues (life, death, nature, "reality") in a "significant" way. But "he" must not speak in any manner that will admit to the historical moment or jeopardize the deepest ethical, political, or metaphysical beliefs, including the inherited discourse we have learned to perceive as poetry.

The thing to remember, as you read, is that *Bloody Jack* is one of many Cooley texts that deliberately set out to undermine precisely these beliefs about poetry. Not to deny them entirely, but certainly to put them to the question. And so it asks us, the readers, once again, what exact construction will we put upon these words, here.

Poetry
The paradoxical question at the core of this text: what is poetry? Whatever we call the writing here, it is very carefully crafted. And when it looks like poetry, it is also a marvellous example of a poet who fully understands the importance of the line break to open form versification. In his essay "Breaking and Entering (Thoughts on Line Breaks)," Cooley argues for the careful use of this formal component of open form, but he also suggests how it can push his own vernacular forward: "This line works with speed. Draws on narrative, idiom, anecdote, repetition ... Think of the breezy, almost smart-ass form it takes in writers like George Bowering and Robert Kroetsch, calling audibles at the line ...." A reader will find this form throughout *Bloody Jack*, but also some lovely small moments of delicacy, also dependent upon the full care given to the rhythm through the line's break.

Why does he insist upon playing the whole field of the page, even more so in the many small revisions throughout the text? One answer again throws the responsibility back on us, the readers:

> Think of where this puts the reader, puts you off? Where it puts the poem. The poet. We set in motion a new series of relations. Realizations. When the new poem comes on line.
>
> A radical de-centering. Away / a way from the poet as prophet. No more metaphor moses. We witness the migration of authority from author to reader. Unauthorized entries, entreaties. Oh, where are you going said reader to writer, said reader to writing. No treaties—an agonistic relationship. Reader as hero, breaking & entering. The end of the poem as private property, of words in service to the previously known, the already named.
>
> Re-focus the model and you value other things. Poem as verb, as event. Match the aesthetics of line breaks with reader-based criticism, which addresses what happens when we move through a text, bit by bit, in some sequence, and interesting things happen.

An invitation to read through this text with as much abandon as its writer once tossed it on his editor's desk, and then kept sneaking stuff back in. Any order of the pieces will do, but within each piece, please pay attention to every smallest motion of words and syllables as they break against the sure line.

Excess

His extravagance: the early gesture of writing what his and Arnason's stories seem to remember as around 800 pages of "stuff" for *Bloody Jack*, dropping the massive manuscript on Arnason's desk, and then watching the comedy of the editor trying to cut it down to what is still seen as a huge size. This time, being in Winnipeg, he couldn't sneak into the University of Alberta Press office and wreak havoc there, but, of course, he already did so with the (re)new(ed) manuscript he finally sent in, and his continuing desire to toss in just one or two more little pieces.

With this re-issue, Cooley has another chance to add, change things, make sure that nothing stays fixed. Re-writing, or is it just re-visiting / re-visioning the original massive manuscript, and presenting a number of new, different pages on which the figures of this tale of times and travails can act out moments of love, lust, violence, comedy, criticism, and who knows what else. More perspectives, some other lyric lie or truth. All of which fit, as there never was a "plot" to this story, just all the materials a determined bricoleur could collect, amass, and then shove together in a wonderfully haphazard (dis)order (well, it seemed fitting at the time[s]). The book is always complete in its incompletion, yet it also, always, changes, and does so with each reader, including the writer again interfering with what was once known as the text.

Desire

As Phyllis Webb once wrote in the first Canadian postmodernist long poem, the one that made possible all the rest, including *Bloody Jack*, she is often sad because all her "desire goes / out to the impossibly / beautiful." Writing, whether it enters the erotic beauty of Webb's poem, or wanders through the cunning linguistics and occasional sweet beauties of Cooley's, is one expression of that desire. As readers, we are offered a chance to feel such desire, in the act of reading. Laughing, angry, miffed, wary, wondering why we should pay any attention to this minor criminal who was sentenced to death, or to the wacky writer represented as writing (about) him, we enter the realm of desire, and the poem, the poems, offer us its possibilities. Here in all its contingent extravagance is that gift.

—DOUGLAS BARBOUR

Sources

Todd Bruce and Robert Budde, "Cooley Dreams His Way into the World: A Conversation." *Prairie Fire* 19:1 (Spring 1998), 50.

Mark Libin, "Dennis Cooley's *Bloody Jack*: What a Young Man Ought To Know: Failing to read Dennis Cooley's *Bloody Jack*." *Prairie Fire* 19:1 (Spring 1998), 104–05.

Robert Kroetsch, "Don't Give Me No More of Your Lip; or, the Prairie Horizon as Allowed Mouth." *Toward Defining the Prairies: Region, Culture, and History*. Winnipeg: University of Manitoba Press, 2001: 211.

Dennis Cooley. *The Vernacular Muse*. Winnipeg: Turnstone Press, 1987.

Bloody Jack

Elements of the fantastic, which never appear in epic or tragic works, crop forth here....Pathological states of the soul, such as madness, split personalities, daydreams, dreams, and death, become part of the narrative....Menippean discourse tends towards the scandalous and eccentric in language. The "inopportune" expression, with its cynical frankness, its desecration of the sacred, and its attack on etiquette, is quite characteristic. This discourse is made up of contrasts: virtuous courtesans, generous bandits, wise men that are both free and enslaved, and so on. It uses abrupt transitions and changes; high and low, rise and fall, and misalliances of all kinds. Its language seems fascinated with the "double" (with its own activity as graphic trace, doubling an "outside") and with the logic of opposition replacing that of identity in defining terms. It is an all-inclusive genre, put together as a pavement of citations. It includes all genres (short stories, letters, speeches, mixtures of verse and prose) whose structural signification is to denote the writer's distance from his own and other texts. The multi-stylism and multi-tonality of the discourse and the dialogical status of its word explain why it has been impossible for classicism, or for any other authoritarian society, to express itself in a novel descended from Menippean discourse.

—JULIA KRISTEVA

• • •

There have not been here only writers hungering for reality and brilliant narrators whose "dazzling" verve carries off a man's head; whatever the degree of guilt of the accused, there was also the spectacle of a terror which threatens us all, that of being judged by a power which wants to hear only the language it lends us. We are all potential Dominicis, not as murderers but as accused, deprived of language, or worse, rigged out in that of our accusers, humiliated and condemned by it. To rob a man of his language in the very name of language: this is the first step in all legal murders.

—ROLAND BARTHES

• • •

> cld fool the bastards
> —BLOODY JACK

. . •

> We know now that a text is not a line of words releasing a single "theological" meaning (the "message" of the Author-God)....Thus...a text is made of multiple writings, drawn from many cultures and entering into mutual relations of dialogue, parody, contestation, but there is one place where this multiplicity is focused and that place is the reader, not, as was hitherto said, the author. The reader is the space on which all the quotations that make up a writing are inscribed without any of them being lost; a text's unity lies not in its origin but in its destination.
> —ROLAND BARTHES

. . •

to Penny

dear valentine

in february
           when the cold cruises past
like a pet gander
              in snuffle of wind
when afternoon light
                stumbles over the house
& the moon
           elbows propped on the window
shimmy-shuffles in to our room
                     on cold hens feet
mercury curls in on himself
              like an intestine
the tungsten frost
          shunts the sky
boxcars startled awake
              & night
ratchets down on us
          with a buzz

& you home
           in yr red toque
leaning like a speedskater
                  into the torque of wind
home at last
         in toque & tongue

then you
      my love you are
the stove
        thaws my rad
you are
        the pump oils my threads
you are the oil can
           melts my rust

the yard

Cool. Ragweed in one corner. A light rain falling. The prisoner enters dressed in standard prison grey. He walks, steadily, toward us, between the 2 guards.

air whistling inside
leg bones like mine shafts holed
the arm muscles tracking thru
stomach melting
food into sugars
pour into darkred tubes
his beard
feeding
slowly
as quartz
old cells burning out
cells freeing new cells
so kids soap bubbles
off wires
hoop in millions
slippery as mud
& his black hair
sledging back
minute
      ly gripping
sun into muscles
locking
sperm

water walking
in its poison
in its carbon
firing

a warm sponge
walking

The distance must be 100 feet. We cannot see his eyes.
He does not look at us. At first. He looks straight ahead.
Each of the guards holds onto one arm, gently.
Walking.

30 feet away. He steps aside, slightly, where a dog has voided, and there is an awkward moment as the 3 men lose step, then regain their rhythm and move on.
10 feet.

Walking.

He is dark and strongly built and the muscles (you can see) are tight in his back.

He pauses at the steps a second, as though he has just got out of bed. As though he is trying to find the grain in the wood, then he climbs slowly and steadily up.

13 steps. 6 inch spikes. fixing the verticals up. he climbing. up. his breath in jars of frost. his footsteps in the early morning.

the new wood sweet and wet so it softens sound. a priest beside him so low and fast we cannot tell. not a word, Krafchenko. between the posts. in front of him, straight at the rope.

rain spotting dark grey dark patches on his shoulders emerging. Mr. McPherson shifts and clears his throat. shiver now. flicks the hair out of his eyes.

then hood the rope quick priest back murmurs faster quickquick christ quick &. taste old spoons in your mouth. you cannot

the air. eggshell air. stiff.

      icecube

           sunk in your chest

new scene: Medium shot.

Pig in a barnyard, behind and to one side three poles standing in a tripod. Closer shot, head on, pig wary. Jack and the kids sneaking, rope in K's hands. Exaggerated caution. Kids: Sshh. Sshh. Finger on lips. Little girl: Oh sshh yourself. Shawn: You just shutup Becky. They start shoving. Jack: Hey, hey. Cmon you guys. Looket this. Gestures to pig. Girl wiping eyes and nose on back of hands, wipes hands on her skirt. Interested. Krafchenko slips up, pig watchful. Makes his way near, throws out a lasso. Pig jumps and squeaks, Krafchenko misses, falls in mud. Close-up on pig's eye, angry. Krafchenko's eye, angry. Kids' faces worried, Penny laughing.

in his tangerine skin

we buried him
in mint condition
on his eyes
two georges
they shone like hens eyes
he inhaled the dark
hhhhgg hhggg
engorged it
a badger breathing
for blood
when we shovelled him in
christ he was a gorgeous man
the eyes were breathing
& shining blood

DESCRIPTION OF KRAFCHENKO

John Krafchenko. Age 33. Height, 5 ft. 10 inches. Weight, 175 lbs. Nationality, Hungarian. Brown eyes. Dark complexion. Dimple on chin. Clean shaven. Walks erect with quick smart action. Well built. Generally well dressed, and has a good appearance. He was a professional wrestler and travelled through this country and through the United States about seven or eight years ago, giving wrestling exhibitions under the name of Patrick (Pearly) Friesen. Krafchenko speaks the following languages: Russian, German, Bulgarian, Italian, Mennonite, and English fluently. He is a machinist and engineer, and can make himself useful about any kind of machinery. He is an expert revolver shot, and will probably shoot to prevent arrest.

aluminum wind

                        in spring sky is sprung
            opens like a mousetrap
there is a wind so grey and so hard it is aluminum
so cold if you stand too close it explodes in small bottles
    lightning slaps the lamp catches
        its breath \ goes out
                  in instant death
        heart is a battery
                  stores the world's susurrations

          shush SHH—ush SH Ush S hh^{h}ush
husssh ush it says ush ^{ush} us

        its enduring suspicions
            closest lamentations

          meanwhile the sky's high blowings
              an alum moon wobbles
            through its circulations
          albumin sky pitted with time
moon a dirigible we have always known
        to be durable in inconstancy
            floats in a churn

though the world may be near
    the end you can hear
where we might have wished to warm
        our shoes
the gravel rolls & crushes
    currents thicken   clog with cold

              i mean there
                    the places where

                          bodies numb & seize
                  the place where hearts softly roar

you with the stars in yr eyes

sex is
not
its not
in the bag
nor in the sack/
neither

    neither is it
    all its cracked up
    to be (
    or not to be
    come i do
    not know
    either / or
    to be either
    to be

        but you
        know & i
        know & o
        tis true so true

    after the big bang
    weve been drifting
    further &
        further

            a   part

they're gonna make a big star outta me

Con man, ladies' man, robin hood, charismatic character, master of guises and disguises (wrestler, preacher, policeman, art critic, dentist)—John Krafchenko, who with flair signs himself "Bloody Jack," seizes the imagination of Manitoba just before the first world war when he leads a glamourized life as bank robber and romancer. Erotic, irreverent, whimsical, by all accounts he is spectacular. He is flamboyant and popular, especially with his own people. They see in him a sympathetic hero who defies the establishment with wit and bravado.

Starting from his small-town origins and his first taste of injustice and adventure, when he runs away after setting fire to the wood shed at the local school, he moves into a flurry of activity, in many countries, until (and even after) he is arrested for holding up the bank in his home town of Plum Coulee and for allegedly killing the bank manager in the get-away. The papers and workplaces are full of reports centering on the crime, the trial, Krafchenko's past, his escape, his romances, and his execution.

The city of Winnipeg is in a tizzy, crowds attend the trial, Krafchenko flirts openly with women who come to court, and some write Krafchenko love letters when he is in jail. The trial and escape are especially interesting because they show something of the presence Krafchenko possesses. He is full of charm and insouciance throughout his preliminary trial, and later, when he is tucked away in jail with no apparent hope, he talks one of his guards and even his defence attorney—he actually does this!—into helping him escape. Once out of prison he manages, with the help of old accomplices, to hide in Winnipeg, as the headlines blare, through days of massive police searches and wild public speculations.

Krafchenko's romantic connection with Penelope Riches, beautiful daughter of a Winnipeg business man, and local schoolteacher, brings her into a series of hold-ups and other transgressions that set the two of them against a prissy and an insensitive ruling class. Their relationship is at once political and personal, so that even as they turn over their takes to the poor, they fall in love—dallying at fairs, in barns, trolley cars, even in the magistrate's quarters.

In the final scene Jack is being taken out to be hung and the movie crosscuts, at an accelerating rate, with an earlier scene when Penny rises from a bench, smiling, to greet Krafchenko, and comes running to him. That scene now reappears in repeated slow-motion, its length growing with each return. She is running, toward, we see in small glimpses. Then, when the trap is finally sprung, we cut to the shriek of a train, its smoke, and then to Penny on the train, alone, reflected in the glass, staring out onto a field of early snow, a red tie in her gloved hand, on her lap. Her reflection in the window, the snowy fields.

the oral tradition

Yeah he had some yap on him that guy. Always waggin. Well, not always, it only seemed like that. Coz he could really string it, eh. Guess he dint say a hell a lot come to think of it, a lot of the time. But boy could he get off a good one once he got er wound up and goin. Pretty soon hed open up itchin with secrets like Mrs. Hagel on the party line or old man Fraser hes got somethin new to sell & not a word of a lie. Everybody tryna get a whiff. Boys sitting round shooting the shit at the Montcalm & hed get flappin away there too for hours & they crowded up on him then like a buncha farmers theyre at a bankruptcy auction guzzlin beer.

Parently he wuz quite the whizz with the ladies hear tell. Story goes he could sing like a goose left out in the cold it come to women. Running round like a chicken with its head chopped off. Yuupp. Quite a song and dance he'd put on, that guy, for the ladies.

Know what's odd bout him, though? Couldn't write. Not a lick. Couldn't write a single word. Cu'nt read neither. Not if his life depended on it. Too bad they dint get some of his stories down. Lot of them. There's a few people know some of them stories still. But don't count on prying them loose outa nobody, they're a little bit embarrassed about this stuff now eh since they made it, you know, some of them are. Got er tied down so tight and proper you couldn't drive a flax seed up their derrieres with a pile driver.

that fateful day

He was dressed in _____.
A _____ man with _____.
He looked as if _____.
For _____ years he had _____ in _____.
_____, and later he _____.

"Hay, Jack! Over here!" He waved and smiled ingratiatingly. He was sitting beside a big guy with a dark droopy moustache and sleepy brown eyes. The other guy, the big one with the lazy eye lids, didn't say anything at first, but he held a microphone and a CBC camera crew in his left hand. "Outstanding!" he cried. "Outstanding Big Fella! I'll say you are a Peasant Rebel, a Desperado, a Primitive Rebel. Robin Hood. This will make *Identities*. I will say you are ear responsible." "I'm all ears," I sd. Eager. "Eerie, you're eerie man."
So I did, I gave him an earful.
I swear.

Mrs. Rhea Morse

This was whenever my late husband, god rest his leather soul, was away with his railway business with his big watch and teeth and this man in a delirium, a positive delirium, would directly come to me. In his deranged hair he would fling his way through my very door, throw himself like a suitcase upon my person and in most importunate and ungentlemanly manner play upon my open hospitality. Sometimes he would hopfrog out from behind curtains. At such times he, frightful creature, clambered over me like a raccoon and squeezed me like an accordion, knowing full well all the time I had, may the Lord forgive me, a soft spot for him, poor boy, and that, accordingly, he could affront me at his pleasure.

Nevertheless, I took him in hand. He, you might be amused to learn, would for his part on such occasions pick his nose while humming loudly union songs. But I never despaired, not once, of one day lifting him up, as I told him, eagerly, whenever I could seize the chance. Oh, I painted a rosy picture for him, all right.

You lucky stiff, I would tease him, winsomely, in imitation of his own off-hand manner in such affairs, having in our intercourse fond hopes of getting, not unexpectedly I might add, a rise out of him. Although, standing there, he would draw my attention time and again to his stylish close-fitting clothes, not once did I notice, rippling beneath them, his fine young body.

Not once did he show guilt for any advantages he might have taken of a lady who, out of Christian charity, nay the deepest promptings of a nature that was, I think, true to her sex, had taken him in out of the cold. Instead, ravaged by goodness knows what species of excess in drink and foul talk, he used the occasion to slip in his vulgar displays of charm which, of course, his rough good looks and certain smoothness of tongue not withstanding, made not the slightest dent in my modest resolve to entertain him in the most hard and trying of circumstances; though I was, to be sure, prepared to put up with a lot in order to secure his position, realizing, as even then I did, how wanting was his upbringing and how promising were his natural attributes.

So, I took it firmly upon myself, come what may, to take the bull by the horns. At such times he could "feel it in his bones" he would say and his eyes would brighten like the brass handles on Jane Casey's tub. I felt certain, somehow, that if I worked closely with him, and if he applied himself as firmly I believed he was able, any shortcomings might soon be overcome. I had every intention of reforming his manner and of turning it into some finer specimen of our beautiful tongue. I felt sure, as did others, that if only he were to be fitted with a nice tie and suit he would become the perfect gentleman.

To be frank I had other motives, I admit, hoping above all to become myself better informed and to improve the standing to which circumstances had consigned me at birth.[1]

When he left I never felt so put upon in my life.

---

[1] It is rumoured that Mrs. Morse was acquainted with Flower and Reid.

in search of John Krafchenko

No, no, it is the same name. But we are not related. Kraw-chenko is the Ukrainian pronunciation. Kraf-chenko is how the Russians say it. And some Ukrainians in Canada. The "f" is an English spelling too.

The word comes from the root "kraw," "krawvats." Tailor in Ukrainian. In English we say "cravat"—the scarf or necktie. There's the Jewish name Kravitz or Kravets. Same thing. We come here, we learn cravats and grammar. In English we would be Tailor with an "i" or Taylor with a "y." Same thing.

There were a lot of Krawchenkos settled in Saskatchewan around North Battleford, but they are not our family. There are a lot of Krawchenkos.

Bloody Jack could really tie one on.

epitaph

                        hear bout Kraf
                                  yup
      got laid
                                        once
too often
                                            too bad
               he was a genital man
really
                            not surprised
     he was well hung

    the
    lucky
     stiff

you have my word

                periodically
they think
they have me
where they want me
that theyve got me
typed the body shouts & glides
is shortened in their head
lines laid out
even as headstones in the prose
the deadlines of the daily press

watch lead articles in every edition
entire entries over written
written over top of what we say
those settings making me
one of their characters

they puncture the paper with commas
and incisive comments from
lawyers & eye-witness reports
underline the horrors they cover

every day i notice them
lined up like ice-cubes
the columns of words
all the accounts
perfectly justified
in periods sentences right
margins subordinate clauses
but i dont
pause dont even
hesitate where they
make the signs

struck by their blows i vibrate
sound as if i were a crystal
bee   i live in the gaps beneath thot
believe in the invisible gasps under print
i learn to hold my breath
hold my breath
in envelopes of air
refuse to be taken in
i am guerilla of brackets
you cant see me on the page
whited out in your eyes
i bristle inside my winter camouflage
parkaed within my unprintable jokes & puns

if you dont keep watch
i will surface under your faces
emerge from under the ice
puffing i will snowshoe
across the fields undetected
snow stinging my face & wrists
i will infiltrate your lines
blow up the frozen grammar
you have dammed like beavers
your marmalade lives nightmared
by rapids & waterfalls
                                    now & then
i will run the blockades of good taste
canoe words that are dirty &
stinking of rum & castor
right into your letters & evening papers

from yr jails & beds
from the edges where you
would gloss me over
write me out of existence
i will shout
to you hard
of hearing

you can here me (bare
ly(on the margins of thot

that is why
to find me
you must read be
tween the lines

diane

                so I
       breathe in the moon
my lips his lips
on them bruised
my brothers
trickle the moonlight
its dark cinnamon
this night this month of
moths and wind
into his mouth
the night blood
filling his mouth with my blood
filling him like a vein

        your eyes
      when they stare
           startled

the October moon
treacles your neck
our broken skin
the air flippers in
and your body starts
the dark swimming
through muscles
through bones
          so
oh my John
in your body
dear god your body
hard in mine
in my body your body blood
we together John

yes joined
in your stiff embrace
and yes in my mouth yes
oh honey in
my wet wet mouth

        in this
the sweet secret
liquid of our night

shapes of frost

leaning against August the fall corn   in full kernels ripened
until the first frost of September   chewed fast like fat white bugs
into the sun-flower fainting in the sky   and slumping in the fields

so earth exposes   its chilly cheeks
and wan October in a huff pours big bottles of gin into the hurry of wind
rubs the rouge off   the moon's warm mouth
flaking pigment off its face   powdering and pock-marking it
then Hallowe'en shoves over half-ton toilets   shaves off the stubble
hoarfrost hurdling the fences   hurts the garden huddled on hard ground

and then the bright air   froze to aethered feathers
the farthered sky anaesthetized   summer's sweaty stab
so stiff ropes of water   grabbed at the gabled roofs
cabled their coldness   close along kitchen walls
and coal pails   piled in the porch
Christmas cobbling joints of cold   bolting them into beams and joists
January grappling quebec heaters   gobbling their hot flutter of guts
and February fisted its frost   fingering windows unfastening floors
winter nailed so hard into studs   the cat froze solid in the oven one night
and babies bagled warm in bed   woke blinking to the bright white
shapes of frost   heavy silhouettes folded
upon lines of dark   around their lanes of dreams

jail / night before

    and
                .lone
.alone standing .
              in the thin
    so : a pin on cold water
                off paper slides/
my window i imagine
  a wafer of light
to those standing outside watching

     .dark. so dark
torque on the clevis
    fisted in yr head
stoneboat inside dragging dragging
along brainpan
                        grates
    /iron/rungs/
bracket
    off yr/
        𝆙
  broken
sock of
    lungbreath
[going out]

        looking out
on. other side : : watch
        close
  small holes of
    red & yellow
  opened in the black
holes other holes
      they are haloes
           boneblue haloes

closing the night
tourniqueted on streetlights
fingersqueezing to varicose
                cold drizzles
into the cone of light
        shivering
a stray mutt sniffs & pisses on
                rubber tires
their tubes of air stonebruised
snakes kids slingshot in september
a dog splashes in the curb
plugged with mud
brown dog digs
& shakes the wet &
ears pop like bones
unlocked from joints

lights in houses when they go
like our lives Yehuda
quietly or suddenly breaking

but in chill rooms of
babies floating
the slippery light
small bulbs still burning
camphor brushes into
their freckled breath
folds into the cold
& fogs the panes
        light blurs
there in the cool
sleeping babies

flutter & shine
children in shells
      the ozone
in smooth glass shells
gently breathing
      the night

                sliver bubbles
                in frog throats
                blown

Benny's Diction

A certain party then made me acquainted with the other man, introducing him to me as one Jack Ryan. We shook hands. I had never seen him before, but I knew, somehow, that I was shaking hands with John Krafchenko, one of the cleverest and most notorious desperadoes in all of Western Canada, someone whom, I was later to learn, would set off a series of events in motion until, by his nefarious action in Plum Coulee, several bright and promising careers would be brought down to irretrievable ruination, innocent children's lives would be darkened, and women's tears would have been caused to flow in bitter torrents. But nothing of that nature was to be seen in our initial meeting. Krafchenko merely smiled. And, funny thing, right from the start he called me Bennie, would always smile that quick smile and he'd call me Bennie, never fail. "Bennie" he'd say "why don we go for a beer? Jus you n me, Bennie," like he was glad to see me or something. No one else ever did. Be that as it may, he acknowledged the introduction in quiet, well-bred manner, that immediately put me at my ease.

midnight waiting in the cold

New Year's Eve
playing "Spoons"
while the coal sighs and
sizzles quietly in the stove
the kerosene lamp flutters and falls
HSHSHshshshs   HSHshsh
against the wall
Bell crashed out at the table
and the wooden spoons
in a line still
standing on end
in the shelf

wooden spoons
5 of them 5
all in one line
stood them there
setting them there
one by one at supper
a hand of spoons & dark
stooped over us

hear giant shadows jerking
their fingers on the ledge
shedding edges of silence
paddling on the other end
in puddles of yellow
Snag rattles & piddles on the linoleum
dreams stuttering
blue across her brain
when she moves winter dogsmell

midnight waiting in the cold
sputter of frost at the lamp window
& the glass cold on my cheek
Benny Bell Penny & me
watching

              : one two three four five
of them/
        us
           wooden spoons
  still on a shelf
    : Benny Bell Laws me Penny
Law makes 5
           5 pennies make a nickel
    1 penny 4 yr
thought yr after her
            I cn tell
    yr leching Laws
  sure you are
 if you were
here

                              & outside
           a moon riddled with acne
the cows in uncle Ivan's barn
given the gift of speech
wanting something awful
to turn the old goat in
       lord the stingy old fart has
       cut us off of our oats for the winter
       you heard us
       & that's it
       that's the last straw
       far's we're concerned

she's out there too charming
Penny Lyn Riches
oh how I miss her

soon's yr back is turned
        out she goes
barges right out into the wind and snow
apt to flake out out there
woman in her shape
right now she's gropin round
in the gusts of dark bangin
into pitchforks and milk pails just
hopin to get a feel of
some bull's balls
she will be married that year
if it is a cow she will stay single
it'll drive er nuts
waiting
     & me

don't get
  carried
away
           just
              take
    it
     easy
          trying to get a handle on things

i'm the one 2nd from right
between Penny nd Laws
                  #4

        & the pigs too they
can't wait to squeal on him
            think that's bad
            that's not all lord
            know what he did
            what he did to us
            last Saturday
            what that swine Ivan did
            dint even shovel the manure outa here
            way he's sposed to
            that's what
            he promised
            well how'd you like it
            how'd you like it to flop around in it lord
            take that kinda shit
                he promised

     spect the chickens
are raisin the very old dickens too
plucky as all get out them chickens and
squawkin on the dirty bugger
& *Ivan will ya quit peckin on me*
for Pete's sake
wouldn't put it past them
not for one minute
them Barred Rocks
eggin on the hogs
sure they are & the hogs they're
kickin up a terrible fuss
raisin one hell of a stink
the hogs are

but loaded with gin
the blue ruin loud in her
bare nekked lady her
legs that shine like glisten

        don't move
              inside a glass jar
  the 4 of us
chilled
waiting in the
       hydraulic of
  silence for
       a spoon
 to fall
Benny's breath
      thin
       & quick then
            Penny back
      at the door again
           in a gut of
    cold turning
         & you hear
   turning you hear
a dull click on the shelf

boating

wishing to hear her
wishing her
      here
her hair red &
        her hands the bones like birds
        how they rise in the blue
        and the green of her eyes
when she comes
a hot wind
swishing inside
fingernailing the mindflesh
the sweat of her neck stings
    her touch leaves
       marks on my back
   raises a hangnail in my thoughts
her sudden weight songing
     my ribs like a glass xylophone

the salt spray of her
voice drawing blood
      draws me
        cisterns of blood

out in my mind

   out of my mind
wishing to hear her
      wishing her
   here

& out back
the backyard of my head
a hunched up crow
like a baby in hunger

shifts & gurgles
it moves & calls
    endlessly
crying & crying
somewhere in the black
that is stalled at the back of my mind
a crow sings something
    i want to hear
something i cant make out

to plum coulee bungling

bang of brandy)chilled
the wrapper
should phone now
randy as a 3-peckered billy goat
ripped loose
yeah hey c mon les stob n phone
before we throw a connecting rod
way the motors bangin

bring to nose brain tongue tired
to hand runs and Penny Penny
warm behind warm be/hind
in bed warm in Winnipeg
bedwarm sleepy lasnight/snoozing Penny

killed the bottle 10 measly ounces

but poppin we like are rattled
      corn man
but brittle beans bumbling
to Plum Coulee bungling

into town like
mangled yes we are
         toms

scared too
no singing
shes cold & hungry
    in spring
bones chewed so bad

not even the bitch
ud touch em
not worth
a pinch of coonshit
    now

Tomson Benny Gardiner Bell nd me
       landing
                  cold & broke

   in spring

the telephone pole

                          is a perfect
            listener it stands & waits
        your call

who would believe these wires
& bulbs would want to wear us

              the pole
       is swaying & shaking
with new sounds
                it is a pillar
     shaken by messages

the wood is crossed by your signals
        sips itself full on you
                it is fueled on
   the electric sap it slurps up
   your field of flesh
         wet with your feeling

        the telephone pole quivers & flashes
its white flesh
    in spasms of light
it hums to those who listen
only to those who glisten
        who sweat in the mud

                at the post
      i am a woodpecker
           trying to tap the code
   trapped like ring
worms inside the tree

                        your voice budding /   building
            in my ear
quavers roundly in the air
            green in my chest

penny's song

Now young Krafchenko long he knew
He had to get a crackin
And so he headed straight for town
To woo and do some smackin
To woo and do some smackin

So Jack come dustin down the roads
And bawled so hard and gaily
He made the crowded streets vibrate
And he stole somebody's baby
Well he stole somebody's baby

How old are you my smirking miss
How old are you my sorrow
Answered back in a cock-eyed grin
Half-past three tomorrow
Be half-past three tomorrow

Well come with me to hooch and smooch
Just come with me my grinner
We'll clip clean over the gumbo flats
Where you never will think of dinner
To a place you'd sooner inner

Now a promise made and a promised maid
They're hard to keep divided
That's especially true when it involves you
And she is firmly decided

She yanked right off her tight-laced corset
It was made of whale-bone grippers
She slipped right on that slinky slink dress
And she rode off in new zippers
They both went off in them zippers

Last night I sank in a soft down tick
Beside my hubbie the dud
But tonight I'll ride in this fast fast car
By the side of my wild Jack's blood
By the side of my wild Jack's blood

And this is the tale of Bloody Jack
And the tale of Penny Riches
Of how he snatched and how she latched
Onto his blue jean britches

the lady with the lamp

am a lantern   feeding on
what lies below me

a line   with a little light
i draw on   the air that beads on you &
around you   open   i like to
think a thimble of warmth
       a small balloon of light

            it is winter lady
            the wind walks in the cracks
            when   the fine hairs where
            your hair stops
            you lean close
       intently looking
            i do not burn
            with a small steady flame
            night after night
               the wind &
the fumes keep
        seeping up
    the flat spine
they are pumped by my terrible need
always   they burn me

i choke with smoke
brim over with the smell
that keeps me going
i suppose you too
film up with it

as i use it up
do i   use you

do i ever   i wonder
crowd upon your air
do i   take your breath away
     even once   do i
rub the fog off your glasses
where your eyes hide
does this   ever happen

in the yellow flutter of my life
when you touch me
if you are not careful
you will burn
your self

when you lean over me
if you are not careful
you will blow
me away

that fateful day

His previous escapades had shown some daring and not inconsiderable cunning, but not this last dastardly crime, perpetuated in broad daylight while the unsuspecting citizens of the little village, who both liked and feared the infamous John Larry Krafchenko and who, even as he pulls up in front of the local bank, are enjoying their noonday meal. It is noon on Monday, May 1st and the streets are nearly deserted, except for a few farmers, and one or two children who are horsing around in front of the bank building. This dastardly crime savored of the boy who had read too many dime novels and who wanted to do something, anything, daring and let everybody else know it was Krafchenko that did it, believing he is shrewd enough to outwit the entire police force and then work his escape. He walks up to the wicket and simply asks for the money, just like that. "Good to see you, Mr. Arnold," he is reported to have said on first entering.

He was always an unscrupulous dare-devil, who would use any one, regardless of consequences, to aid and abet his notorious schemes. But the unlooked for happened. The shot he fires kills one Mr. Henry Medley Arnold, choir-master in a local church, and ill-starred manager of the Bank of Montreal in Plum Coulee, and to my mind, from what I have seen of Krafchenko, I do not think he meant to shoot with fatal result. In a steady voice Mr. Arnold asks Krafchenko to get off the bank property, to quit the premises quietly, or words to that effect, and you can imagine where that would have got him with a person of Krafchenko's state of mind. It would not of been a real bank robbery if he had not fired off his gun. And then he might have meant to instill fear in the citizens. It is well known among police circles in the province that he was a good marksman with a pistol, always carrying a brace of them.

But if his acquaintance with anatomy had of been as fit as was his aim, Mr. Arnold might never of got himself killed. Krafchenko had posed as a doctor several times (under assumed names this was), but it was not fated he should see the steel-jacketed bullet entering the soft part of the shoulder is to swerve severely down and away from the shoulder blade, way around the neck, and lodge in the ring bones of the vertebrae. The result being to sever the spinal nerve and thus bring instant death.

behind the muscles

        saw:
            bones
  was:
      a barn of muscled bones
        a bone of blood
hanging
in the clean oil
in the nightcotton
      where they shine

      moons razor
        zzztt   zztt
          hones on the cold
   wheels of wind
& rain
   a carborundum sky &
     the winds deboning

          unbottling
the arms hips this chest
    pared
   to a hyphen to commas swung
     in nights serration

         then the tongue
   beheaded
     its U bone
       chipped
          free
    flips
/flips
     in my silent mouth
  a jewel
     grasshopper
      earring the night

        rain & wind
      when they rub
          my bones they rub
the linseed dark
       the emery cloth wind

                the mute bones
       my rib bones
           on its wet
     gravel faces
          tumbled smooth
       as air in agate

        when they blow
            in the morning
              to carbon
   turning
            my heel bones
they are   running
    slippery with rain

strobic flies

                      floors stuttering
    movie
        people
            flick past/
                      strobic flies/
                                flick/
                flick/
     flick/
                        flick/
           white
              curtains parted
                    flaking off
   dark ribs of men

   & rubber suns they are
   balls bouncing off
   walls & ceiling
   bounce as i turn
   my crystal wrist

liquidclicks his tongue Doug
slicking down yr hair
as he combs & cut
    combs & cuts
pock marks in his wet voice
    at the sticks
bodies in jerks & clicks

you watch the kid waiting
    he's next
picking his nose
wipes it on his sleeve / torn
picks his nose & crayons a book

damned if he doesnt have one of these
big balloons
air packed tight as
one of Pennys tits &
like one of her nipples
pinched & darker on the end
spits sunflower seeds)draggled bugs on
floor pitted by the rug
kid with rust hair
whistles in bright air
in bright that whistles
                      by the clothes rack
                                    fidgets & colours

light lingers

        me here &
     light lingers/
            bright fingers on
          lift of your breast
   dress fallen
)open
     on half turning
                skinnaked
         by the window
                blind
       one arm above you thin
        and your hand
               left in your hair

bare

   : a picture
        of you
  in my head
     crisp as celery
  in summer's smudge
the hot drizzle behind
      all round you
  burning into
          the grey/green of your eyes
      in the picture
           fading now
    still
  more green than they're grey
                looking out/into
        the room where we
            (locked) liking
        what you could see
       what could you see
       what do you see out

        there these
            2000 miles

          how many
                miles
                    kitetail snapping
                        on your mind

noticing now
    later
  as i dig out
      the picture
          the cool round of
              your earrings
                    (smile
                  quick coming
      their delicate
           green
              & red
smell of sunwarm cotton
here as i wait
    in the drained
        other sun other red
      a silent fall

          a brown paper bag
          the kid is blowing up

Rex v. Krafchenko

Gentlemen, there is no room in the jury box any more than there is on the Judge's bench for weak sentimentality. The duty may be stern, it may be even repugnant to our natural feeling; but it is a duty which must nevertheless be honestly and fearlessly faced. The common jury has long been regarded as the palladium of British liberty, and it will hold that high place in public confidence just so long as it can be depended upon, in the language of your oath, a true verdict to give according to the evidence. The security of life and property depends largely upon the integrity and fidelity of jurymen. For the law as it stands neither you nor I have any responsibility. It may be that some of you might like to see it changed. It may be that a better system of dealing with those found guilty of capital crimes might, in your opinion, be adopted. But for the time being it is the law of the land and you and I are bound to give it effect. I am not saying this to you because I suspect for a moment that any of you would be guilty of the weakness of refusing to return a true verdict because of the consequences to the accused which might follow. I believe you are one and all duly impressed with a sense of the great responsibility that rests upon you—a responsibility to the public, to yourselves, and to your families—and if you think the prisoner guilty of the crime charged against him you will by your verdict say so, regardless of the consequences.

laying down the law

look either we stand up and be counted or else the little grubber lights out again the little creep will just up & skitter out right from under out noses & wherell that leave us. well get caught with our pants down we wasnt looking. sames last time. make fools of us. agen. ya want that to happen agen him make A-1 assholes outa all uv us. ya want that do ya. no i dint think so.

well then lissen pay attention you lisnin Lenoski rest of you guys hes no great shakes no hell comes right down to it scrubby little bush-whacker like that. shit gainst men like ourselves & cant draw flies to shit no more. come on now you men all know that sos why ya all lookin like a gaggle of girls ya stept on their toes or somethin. Reimer ya know hes just some kind freak the Lord got screwed up somethin awful makin. & ya better believe it he met his match this time. so lets move now no way we lay back & stand for it this here little shrunken ape come knockin yur back is turned & then there he goes & hightails it outa here the little prick showin us his heels.

you all heard the scuttle butt you got wind of it every one of ya. all them hussies in town themthere blowzy dresses tittight whadda they see in him anyways 'sif he got a knack for it or somethin just twitchin theirs this way & that way all over the place lord everywhere ya go its scandalous is what it is painted & rollin the eyes all white all over like moanin Daves heifers in heat & he bawlin his head off whole towns just steamin & streamin with the crazy bitches swarmin perspiration & rubbin yuv seen it rubbin rightup against him whimper & quiverin. & thats just fine with you.

Al Al Anonymoz you know a little French words you think we should go tits up on the sidewalk no go on go ahead you think mright just say so. unn uhh. things get hard enuff we just get a grip on ourselves & we put up a united front. we always have we always will. you in Hughes?

JesusJesusJesus how long we got to put up with its gone past all reason this twaddle. sure yur hot under the collar I cn see how yuh feel I know what its like. & so heres what we do. we string him along till he got enuff rope to hang himself we set the booby trap. that there Rich woman shes got him by the nose right. so we move in. fast. we get in there & catch 'm with the pants down. we spring the trap. snap er right tight on that twitchin little hairy tail of his snap er right off.

        right.
put an end to that claptrap.
for good.

i wldnt breathe a word

the prospects as i came upon it
were truly sublime the view
so inviting who would not
have been moved such that i did believe
the world i visaged presaged something grand
bliss was it in that dawn to be alive
but to be in this was very heaven
and thought then to enter that joy
such as might move & give rise to
the most intense feeling
it was one might say
a brush with divinity

a lot you got one hell of a lot JK
you got a lot of nerve mister
threatening to pull out on me
me who has shown you the burning bush
the moment of vision the shores of paradise

honest to god patty you dealt me a severe blow you know
when i fell for you i mean i was prepared
to do darn near anything
id put up with your antics night & day
just between you & me
i stuck my neck out for you lady
way out if you want to know
i got pretty light-headed for a spell there
hissing & hersing away non-stop
wuz an overfilled gastank & i got dizzy breathin
the fumes when you got all worked up
i suffered from a splitting headache

oh don't talk nonsense marlene get off it
it was only a glancing blow

you know darn well i hardly got a glimpse
i was under a lot of pressure
surely to christ she could shrug it off

                         no i cannot
    shrug all you want
you've lowered yourself in my eyes you really have

what the hell's that sposed to mean
what else could i do spot you put me in
me i damn near drowned myself for you
may well have suffered brain damage for want of air
didn't hear nuthin then bout me bein too long-winded
flap though i did like a goddamn weathercock

but no i could howl like the seven
winds at the old inn door
bess i would stand on my toes & call
                     'ts me bj
    just in from the sloughs
& there you'd be hollering your head off
                hollering for more
day in and day out i huffed & i puffed
till i felt like a bellows at dying embers
but do you remember that cinder ella
i mean i was a scuba diver for you
i went to the bottom of the sea for you
sometimes i got sea sick suffered from motion sickness
there i was squiffing away like a can of aerosol a paddlewheel
that's picked up a stiff tail wind thought for a moment of turning
into a whirlwind hurricane a typhoon a strong high wind a blust a
flurry if only for you gale my love
i would have been stormy weather
& there i was comin up with nitrogen in my veins my ears popping

this dear eloise was nothing to sneeze at
you dear darlene were driving me around the bend
& up i came i came up like a beached whale
wheezing for air thair he blows
you cried & you shook
a harpoon in the sky
cried like a harpie

flatly she is

                    i am
          impressed

          i really am
believe me this is something else

                    there at the cpr turnoff
                        rain has passed by
                    a penny   pressed by a train
                      one a penny two a penny

                        penny left behind
     , again

                              says he's
                        got to be gettin' on

              don't spend it in one place
                  he says when he sees
                     my startled face

                              stresses the word it

           no i say
        i won't
you can bet your bottom dollar
                      i won't
            i certainly won't

          talk about pound wise
                              penny foolish

an envelope for penny

        penelope
          ne   e
        pen
        pe   p
         e el
              ope
        pe el
        pe e
        p   ope
        pe e p
         e e   p
        p   op
          n o
          n ope
           lop
      p   lop
          lo
          lope
           elope

o pen i say
          pen
                   ulti
     mately
                       she will
penelope i mean
              pen L.O.P.
                    I will face the muse
                     sick with longing

they have cross words

for you, dear reader—

Across

1) where he grew up (10)
4) his lady fair, of Odyssean fame (8)
5) what shone on them (3)
8) a copper a lover a diminutive (5)
9) what speaks deeply to her (6)
11) crossed sticks, their secret messages (9)
16) his name, really (10)
18) Krafchenko is one, so is crow (6)
19) to woo, a place of judgment
20) a loss of breath (5)
21) where they put him (4)
22) what he moved across, toward (7)

Down

1) what Arnason did for Cooley (5)
2) living by their wits, their passions (7)
3) where it was written, as it ended (8)
6) you, dear reader (6)
7) less than erratic, all she bargained for (6)
10) arraigned / railed against him (4)
12) upon which they hung her hopes (8)
13) where B) iater reappeared (7)
14) what he lived in, what they ended (9)
15) what they did (9)
17) doing what comes naturally (7)

a night out

                    I

on the street car
tuesday after noon
slumps on us
like vaseline glues
flies & blisters on the heels

bluster of tobacco smoke
& the close sweat
office girls get on at eatons
little streets of dirt where
their necks leak heat
the moisture faints on their lips
smeared with desire

sun sucks up throat juices
        snorts it up
the white heat in nostrils

day rides off in a red wind
in grit & tired horses

sun in haemorrhage
spots the flannel

                    II

home to onions & stoveheat
animals shoving & crowding
the way cats can burst a room
& my landlady's sausage with the skin
busted & spitting blood

III

light slides to rum
night dresses in black & pearls
in saxophone & trombone loosens
cramps of street lamps
open like babies' fists
discharge the light

in times like these
you are a tube of electric water
wet with neon

in pearls slippery
from nicotine

let out our breath

IV

falls back
to the ground
morning unzips
white with skin
one eye in the head
aches like aspirin

a transformer
it hums & hums

V

        but i wuz up
        at the crack of
        a sparrow fart

im squeezing the sun

im squeezing the sun
a blob of blood
squashing the sun
tight with mosquito blood

with blood in its throat
sun in its bubbles of blood
its hunger song

is holding it
in a milk bottle
they cant tell if it bites
they cant tell it is stings

it hunts after night
in rattle of heat
kills with its heat pits on fire
with its skinned eyes of blood

love in its eyes
love in its whirr of flesh
its mouth
swims in my blood

biter of blood
sun in a clear
bottle i put you
wanting it so
and i am sure
no one can tell
if i let it bite
if i let it sting

WHAT HAPPENED
WEEKS EVENTS IN REVIEW

Not even the most reckless adventure could begin to match up to what has happened over the past five weeks. Events have simply ravished the imagination of citizens to a fever pitch. The episode of Krafchenko's escape, the sensational climax of it all, has had the same effect on the public mind as a torch applied to an open tank of kerosene. Such has been the melodrama that has galvanized Winnipeg.

Intoxicated with the role he was playing, Krafchenko, in a flamboyant display of bravado, sneered at the police throughout his preliminary hearing. He grinned non-stop, all the more as his part in the damning story about the murder unfolded. Whatever his true feelings may have been at the mass of evidence that brick by brick was being stacked against him, "Kraf," when something amused him more than usual, would glance around the court with a childish pride in the relation of the circumstances, no matter however good evidence was against him. "Kraf" appeared thoroughly to enjoy the tilts between counsel and to invite admiration from the audience.

One story typified the almost unbelievable wildness of the Plum Coulee native. According to Albert Bell, a Winnipeg friend of Krafchenko, "Kraf" had after the actions in Plum Coulee deliberately sauntered right past the North Winnipeg Police station under the full glare of lights shoving from the building and joked about it as he went. That's how certain "Kraf" was that "they can't tie one on me."

Apparently, when the defendent was still at large he had consolidated all the fixings in order to disguise himself as a woman—a wig, coat and skirt, petticoat, large-sized shoes, imitation Persian lamb muff and throw, shirt waist, felt hat, gloves, veil, talcum powder, cold cream. The works. These preparations show how careful the outlaw was to secure his escape. Yet it was learned, the defendent actually went out into the streets in costume, lunching in Eaton's and hitting the night life generally. On one encounter, which brought laughter from the court, he very nearly got himself picked up—not by a burly police officer, but an amorous sport who had had one too many.

Ironically, quite a large number of women were in court through the proceedings, an unprecedented occurrence at the city police court. On one or two instances Judge Mathers was forced into reprimanding some woman, so aflutter was she. Whether such women were stricken with the pathos or the adventure of their hero is hard to ascertain, but one thing is certain: they seem to have been touched on the raw. Therese Reigie, crown witness, seemed hostile to the crown attorney after being some time on the stand and could not remember anything of import about Krafchenko. Throughout her testimony she would steal glances at defendent until finally she was enjoined not to do so and thereafter she laid off.

In the end the weight of evidence stashed the romantic character behind bars where he awaited trial. His outrageous threats and flippancies could not save him. Or so it seemed then. Who would have thought even as court sat he could have broken out that very night? That, even as counsel spun out the tale of his shocking crimes, he was plotting to "fly the coop"? But he did. Waving a gun smuggled in to him by Percy Hagel, defence counsel, rhythmically at his guards, Constables Reid and Flower, he breathed threats interlarded with oaths. In no time at all, he was out.

Fastening a clothes line no bigger than a woman's ring finger to a window in the photography room, he made his move and swung out. But the rope snapped 30 feet from the ground and the inmate was severely crippled. Buxton later testified how both hands were ripped to the bone, the ankle had puffed up twice the normal size, and the knee cap had burst.

The press and the police, even Mayor Deacon, were stormed with anonymous letters supposedly penned by "Jack" himself. If the great variety of chirographies on these missives were any sign a hundred Krafchenkos infest these parts. The escape was made material for poems and puns and uncountable spasms of verse. Some were very good and some very bad were received by the papers. One poet, crazed evidently by the bandit, went so far as to write an entire book. Many other compositions were abuzz with rumours about "Jack's" whereabouts, as the giddiness sprinkled through the nation like fire in grass.

For days, the police were dumbfounded and red-faced. It was as if the most magnetic character in all the annals of Manitoba crime had simply flown out through the night in a biplane and pulled all the clues with him. They had no clues. They make no arrests. Speculations abounded. The amazing escape breathed new life into the simple fans of the criminal who were agog with new thrills.

After days of desperate forays, the case was to be broken open. John H. Buxton squealed under pressure and from there on it was only minutes until the dangerous outlaw was flung safely into incarceration and his little adventure was over.

The arresting party was led by Chief Macpherson, after days of chaff and badinage, wanting to avail himself. It was feared, needlessly, that the hot-blooded "Kraf" would kill to avoid capture. The fears were without reality, as the bandit was savagely incapacitated from injuries taken on in the fall. They caught up to him in the Burris block, 686 Toronto, at 11:04 p.m. In the pitch dark someone struck a match and as the light flushed up Macpherson stepped forward into the pool.

"Jack, play square and we will give you a square deal." He drove the words home like nails in Krafchenko's coffin.

"All right," laughed Krafchenko, dead game in his condition.

To which the Chief, or someone else at the site of arrest replied, with relief, "It's a wonder you did not kill yourself."

Here the story took on a human interest turn.

Though Krafchenko had given Chief Macpherson endless trouble, the chief's attention to his prisoner was more than ordinarily careful. In fact his whole endeavour was to save Krafchenko unnecessary pain. Krafchenko walked out of the suite, and along the landing, when the Chief noticed "Kraf's" leg appeared to be giving him intense pain.

"Get on my back Jack," said the Chief, "and I will carry you." Or words to that effect.

When they had descended one

flight, the Chief paused for breath, and Mr. Stodgill made a motion to come forward to relieve him. "I'll manage to walk the rest now Chief," said Krafchenko, and he limped the rest of the way with the aid of Chief Macpherson and Eli Stodgill.

Arrived at the sidewalk, Chief Macpherson noticed the large limousine in which the Free Press had followed the police. Turning to one of the Free Press representatives he said: "Can I have your car? Krafchenko will be more comfortable in it."

The reporter gave his assent, and Krafchenko was assisted in, Eli Stodgill going first to pull him in, while Chief Macpherson remained on the sidewalk. Gingerly Krafchenko stretched his injured leg over the back of the seat in front of him. When he had completed his preparations, Krafchenko remarked in an easy manner: "O.K. Now I'm nice and comfortable. Ready to go Chief?" And he winked at the crowd watching. They hung over the car like broccoli.

Krafchenko's right hand was swathed in amateur-looking bandages. He had a gold "snake" ring on the little finger.

Despite the fact he was in excruciating pain, he never let the cigarette which he stylishly held go out.

The whole attitude between Krafchenko and the Chief was much more reminiscent of a strong man aiding an invalid friend, or a younger brother, than of a chief of police conveying a desperate criminal and jailbreaker to custody.

When Jack Krafchenko fell on the breaking of the rope, by which he made his memorable escape from the central police station in the wee hours of the night, he received injuries that are very likely to prove serious.

Dr. Jack Lewis-Smith, provincial jail physician, examined the prisoner yesterday at the jail, and found that he had one painful injury.

Krafchenko apparently alighted on his right heel from his long drop, and this portion of his foot is hurt badly and jammed, and it may be a long while before he will walk again. His right ankle is seriously wrenched, and his right leg is hurt.

The injury most to be feared is in his back and neck, and the result of this might be paralysis of the leg.

It is impossible for a few days to know definitely just how seriously the nerves have been impaired by the terrible impact of the fall to the hard pavement. The doctor thinks he might never be the same again.

Krafchenko's general health is said to be fairly good, although there are evidences that he has not lived as carefully as he might have done.

In any case, things are back to normal and the dubious hero is fastened down now for good in a second storey iron cell overlooking the university, where he once "taught." But he continues to display his overpowering egotism and daily spins his wild fairy tales. Fantasies of diamond caches, Australian gold in great chests, beautiful women who sought him in Vienna and kept him in New Orleans, and the ease with which he would have escaped had he not been injured were uttered boastfully. Flagrant lies, every one of them. Police at the provincial jail were agog at this audacity in elaborating such accounts. But they all claim to a man he tells "some pretty good ones."

What is a wonder still in the story is how "Kraf" could talk so many people—Buxton, Holt, Reid, Hagel, Westlake (the latter two employees at Security Storage where the injured escapee holed up the first night)—into supporting him so suicidally in his ill-fated escape. They seem to have been infected by the mania that clamped itself onto the public mind. In each case those who abetted "Kraf" acted in no hopes of gain. They too seem simply to have been mesmerized by the bandit and to have fallen under the spell of his charm. He was simply fascinating.

birds of a feather

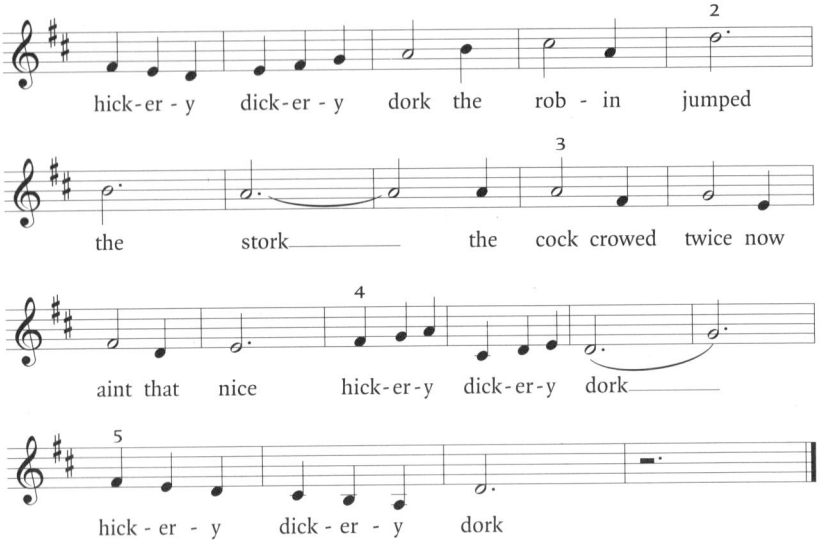

crow contests

                      sun says oh yeah
             think you can just go ahead & try
             let's see you try tough guy
                      you're so smart

         crow is quite a hunk
         crows swells up real big & laughs
big laugh   **hahh hhhahhh**
tree shakes when crow laughs
       nothin' to it
    stupid sun you got
    no goddamn brains

me? says sun. you talkin' bout me?
you crow you ain't got two cells
to rub together
yr stupid as a post

            yeah says crow
            its all in here

                  all of it? in there?
                  sun pokes crow in the belly.

     yeah all of it

         ok sun says
      waitamminit i got an idea
         watch this

                      sun climbs up
                         the tree real
slow and sun gets
             hotter &
     hotter climbs

        the poplar leaf
                by leaf & they flutter
     like hankies people shade
                  their eyes & start
        to point hey what's that
crazy sun doin'

   crow snorts
   he's not impressed

        sun starts to get red
            in the face don' say
   nothin' just
      climbs & climbs
          face gets redder & redder
    crow laughs & laughs
pumps himself up & down on the branches & hollers
stupid sun you ain't got an ounce of sense

crow is getting hoarse
      from laughing & pointing
      sun jus' keeps on a climbin'
      after a little more crow
         starts to get   dizzy
            the air is rattling in his ears
      his sight blurs he begins to slur

crow thinks it is time to slow down
        climbs into the tree & sits down
        maybe he will stay there for a bit

crow lets go a few more curses
that the best yuh kin do sun
hopes to sound coarse & derisive

           meanwhile sun is way up
        past the tree now
        & crow hunkers in
        sweating like a pig
           lower still gets pretty quiet
         don' say much no more
hopes he can stick it out

     by now crow is
    too limp to glower
    sees only smears in the hot air
            the sun is slippery with sweat

              and then
              sun has had enough
              calls it quits & begins
              hand over hand
                        starts to
          climb
     back down
        smooth as a snake

by the time sun reaches the other side
looks into the tree crow has let himself
        way in and crow
               wobbles on the branches
   sun peers in until
                 the whole tree shakes &
  crow
          flops out
    flaps like a dying chicken
barely hears when sun softly
       plops at the bottom

crow hacks and groans
crow is plenty scared
sky turns
the colour of mustard plaster
crow heaves and vomits
shits red all over the horizon

the facts

- escaped Jan 10, 1914
- through the frame of a photograph
- it was in a photography room
- in the jail
- he had a key
- using a smokeless Colt 32 automatic
- he quickly developed in the dark room
- helped by
  - John Buxton
  - John Westlake
  - Robert Reid
  - Percy Hagel
- he had a rope
- Hagel was probably drunk, got the wrong rope
- the rope broke and he fell 30 feet
-
- it was bitterly cold
- his heel was severely damaged and it is not known when or if it will fully heal
- badly maimed he was picked up by joy riders
- limping he was picked up by Percy Hagel
- people from Plum Coulee still remember him, so do many from Winnipeg
- he went to the Burris Block on the corner of Toronto and Ellice
- he went to 546 William posing as a doctor
-
- he went to 439 College Ave pretending to be a poet-professor from St. John's College
- on the way he spoke German Ukrainian Russian English French Hebrew Polish Hungarian Spanish, he being a master of language
- he stopped passers-by to quote long sections from a book called Bloody Jack
- he also escaped from the penitentiary in Prince Albert by abandoning a painting brigade

- he was a professional wrestler boxer steam fitter temperance lecturer known for his fiery and evangelical zeal blacksmith forger locksmith womanizer machinist gambler bank robber bigamist con man freight-handler shape-shifter escape artist lock-picker in England Russia the United States Australia Italy Germany he being a master of guile and guise
- he was everywhere, there were reports of him in Brandon, Calgary, Ontario, England, reports flowed in
- he was nowhere, nowhere to be seen
- the police collared him on Jan 19, 1914
- he was armed to the teeth at his aunt's home, 133 Barber St.
- he gambled and drank with his pals at the Moose Club and the Pyramid Club
- he went under many aliases, among them Pearl Smith and Tommy Ryan
- when he was 14 he had an affair with his father's mistress, whereupon his father shot himself in the foot
- 70 witnesses appeared at the trial
- which ran from March 18 to April 9
- 10,000 people signed a petition for clemency. 20,000, some said, and it weighed 12 pounds.
- some believe that Ben Rolph betrayed him to the police. Rolph says no, someone called Bert Bell put the finger on Krafchenko and pointed out the house where he was holed up.
- the mayor said "it will be impressed upon the criminal element of the foreign population that under British Law it will be extremely unhealthy to indulge their propensities in the direction of the city"
- a local minister said he should step on the gallows and die like a man
- there were 120 witnesses and Crow Prosecutor W.H. Hastings provided as many exhibits
- his mother in Greece was a notorious horse-thief, who would go away dressed as a man and come back as a woman with many horses
- he himself thought of dressing himself as a woman and escaping from Winnipeg in disguise, even bought an entire wardrobe

- it was his step-mother, actually, who believed in warlocks and witches—she tried to revive him by breathing into him
- he entertained thoughts of leaving town in a coffin
- he left in a plain coffin and was buried in an unmarked grave in lot 546, section 22 of Winnipeg's Brookside Cemetery
- the gun is in an old shoebox in police custody. It was manufactured in Hartford, Conn, in 1912. Someone has filed the serial number off the barrel, but they missed it underneath the grip. 137742. The initials J.H.B. are cut into the handle.
-
-

- he flipped the hair out of his eyes and smiled just before the hangman slipped the hood over his head
-

- the letter said "I would go but for my wife and three children and give myself up. I am the guilty one. You did not give me away. I am leaving for parts unknown. Will say God be with you—a man on earth is a man in heaven."
-
- her name is Fanica
- her name if Fanicia
- he was 34

the script

                            watching
        to the clerk's pen
            it goes
     skritch skritch
                  skritchkritch
skritch
          a chicken toe nailing mosquitoes
       inside the paper's throat
                 my words getting

             into the hard paper that crunkles
                  when you turn it
      over
the reporter too   taking it down
    short hand
       looking up
                a quick flick of his eyes
      nicking flies out of the heavy air

                    my words out of the sound
                        drawing them from where
         they roar like a toaster
                   his pen
           stroking fast
       all the sounds muffle
     into ink as it sprawls
         down crawls through layers and
                  layers of
       pulverized trees
          faintly trembling
     the black pen
      the paper
        running out steadily into
            running down
                 the sheets

                lying there
                        crisp & white
                as an English virgin

                                Penny   3rd row
                                            windowlight hitting
                                her eyes now &
                                        then / way wind crinkles water

                        the men's faces
                                    on oak benches
                    screens blot over
                                    their eyes
                            they conscript what is said
                                            all the talk left
                            hanging
                    the footings
                                kicked out from under
                so when I speak it
            is papering the walls of their mouth
        the rooms of their ears
            so clogged with wax
                            my voice roams
    back to me
        in burnt cigarettes
                                    strangely altered
                            puzzling them out
                        over coffee and muffins
                            in next day's paper
                                    & the letters i get
                            in childish lettering
                                        frayed envelopes

                         fragile stationary
afraid/   they speak of love &
                              god
              she
                  of cold & kids
                  names in Xs and Os
          I've never seen

slow fan over us/
              lolls
          Hagel's hands
              wet in the heat
                       blotching
              in notes where
                  his hand
                              stains

    fish flies on the waterskin
they moisten & soft
                   begin to run
                       to run & tangle
                          silence in the courtroom

                  Pennys face
          her face collapsing
          like towels in a washtub

       the clerk coughs & scratches
       & in the register too
                   varicose veins in the trans
                       cript they read
                              straining
              god's entrails
              fingers touching

                        the crazed insides
            of god his secret
                        teaching
                                    as if they could
                describe
                                they
            would decipher

                        & when
                they come   the scribes
                        in black
        to see
                the carbon
copy of my words where

                    will i be
            what they read here
                        in jangled yellow
            my loud venal sins like deerflies/
                                    embalmed
                lies penned up in their
                                false
        teeth
                all that's left

                    the signatures bound
                together not worth
        the paper they're written on

                        & me i wonder
                will i be
            will they be
all of them
            writing me

            off in a series of strokes
                  in their stiff post
script some odd cipher
                     in their hands

            no one to hear me
                here

                              in time
            my teeth busted
      loose

                        in the used air
                all their bite
                              gone

Barn. Camera low.

On screen sunlight lancing through cracks in barn, dust in the bars, sound of chickens. Voices, off camera, muffled, excited. Camera pans through the slats of light, dust in them, finds Jack and Penny in the hayloft. They backlit from frame of door in loft, side by side. Behind them a rope on a pulley, for lifting hay. Camera low, close-up, no talk except for the sounds of bodies in the hay, and the animals in the barn. Their breathing (sound up). Naked bodies in partial silhouette & soft light, carry a halo of light. Close-up.
Penny: Jack?
Jack: Hnnmm?
Penny: Well ... you know .... Shawn ...
     Jack: Yeah ... he's a good kid ...

in the park

Saw him again, today. At the Hjartarson Cafe. And forgot my purse and had to go back next day and get it. Thank god she wasn't there. Ran into him in the park by Probert's place. I was strolling the baby like I have all summer. In my new lawn dress this time. And such a fine day. Sunshine freckling onto the ground smell of cut grass and the sprinklers throwing spindles of light up into the air. Sun like brandy and the orioles and robins all excited. And I was thinking of him, then, the last time we met, him and me. Clouds of mosquitoes at the fair and I find him near the freak tent peeking *hurryhurryhurrysteprightupfolks* at all the passer-bys out of the corner of his eye. But Danny's messed his pants and he gets cranky so I take him to the room there in the park. So hot then I think maybe I will have a lemonade. Mrs Horner, lady from the flat next door, says sure she'll look after the baby for awhile I should just go and have some fun my hands so full all the time, for a change. So away I go for lemonade. Well, who should pop up just then when I'm lined up? But there he is that same laughing in his eyes like everything is funny only he likes it too. And I am so nervous all a sudden I can hardly look at him so excited to see him I must be shaking so bad everyone can see and he with those eyes and his smile my god I feel like when I patted that horse that time at the fair or something way I am so ascared and so quick. And the sun keeps on running rainbows in the sprinklers and those eyes. He says sure come on lets get a drink and me so scared but why not when do I see him and Danny's fine Mrs Horner said don't worry and so I can hardly catch my breath that sounds like a good idea. Streetcar to the cafe way cross town and me sitting beside him all the way laughing and talking. And he all the time so close I can smell him. I can touch him, John. Hardly knowing if I'll get back in time. Or caring. Don't worry. Same thing at the cafe. Can't think of what I want and he asks for two lemonades. And all I can think is him and me there and the waitress watching and a beautiful woman with long brown hair she called Eva looking at us and drawing but who cares and oh my John I wish I could I wish we could and do you really if my stretch marks and those others so young and oh my body starting to sag like his balloon do you John do you really if with your eyes the sad in them too and your black hair and life in you like an orange would you then even then would you would you

flame swallower

a bottle factory on the graveyard shift
        you light up
crimson in your pipes & hoses
your tubes like neon
signs at a pizza parlour
all the bones by
oranges & yellows bent
your liver turns
into a smoked goldeye
your glass brain a bulb
snaps on like a headlight in fog
& your eyes turn to kids marbles
clear as electricity
far as eternity

meanwhile the blue halo
DTs round your dirty hair & fingernails
& you all the while squawking & croaking & shaking
a plastic parrot in fever

then you open
your mouth in pain
you a gas tank and *ahh*
        it whooshes
we gasp ten feet tall
fall back in the molten air
scorches the roof of the tent
the roof of your mouth burnt
all the beautiful words
vomiting over us
the lava acetylenes
down on our heads
fire works / fire words
getting onto our hair

into our eyes
catching fire
wild in grass
in eyes of smoked glass

breaking up is hard to do

            looklook   hes break
                              ing the line
                2 feet from the end
a full 5 metres from the and

      he just broke
        a word in two
      did you see that boy
      he must be
  strong
          flexible too the way he just up and
              bends at those joints
                    lotta people cant even touch their toes
but hes so articu
          late
     ly stringing a line

my god she sd
my god sd she he must be
      writing a big book
         this time
              am not sd he

no hes not hes gonna fall
& break his neck/ the fool
sd Ann if he doesn't
stop this fooling a
      (round)
        if he doesn't
     watch his
          step

corvus brachyrhynchos

a chunky bird
related to the blue jay and the magpie
totally black except for
a blush of bluish or greenish sheen
concentrated on its wings back and tail
its bill and feet are strong and black
the eye is dark

an opportunist in its feeding
it will eat almost anything
weed seeds garbage grasshoppers field mice baby birds frogs oats gophers
crickets dead skunks ducks eggs dogs on manure piles plums humps of fat
corn ants snakes live and dead sunflower seeds squashed porcupines
chopped off chicken heads cow pies run over cats frozen robins starved
meadowlarks rats diseased orioles grounded spiders cows entrails pig shit
cold porridge steers testicles horse buns capsized pigeons stored wheat
rotten pumpkins blue flies bean sprouts washed up fish slow mice run over
weasels mangled gophers stale bread spoiled potatoes sick kittens slugs
rabbits grapefruit rinds squirrels with broken necks kidneys of lame horses
lungs of tubercular sheep turnips left in gardens carrot peelings young
chickens ladybugs fresh dog turds fishflies saskatoons acorns chestnuts
cheese afterbirth skunks smeared on roads eyes is especially

fond of eyes
in legend and in fact
it pecks out the eyes of hanged men
almost anything that catches its eye
highly adaptable and resourceful
is capable of occupying
a great variety of habitats
it even scrounges on the fringes of cities
in the winter congregates
around garbage dumps and slaughter houses
where its coarse shouts can always be heard
above the other birds

much maligned as a nest plunderer
"a dozen nests may be found
occupied one day and destroyed the next"
and tormenter of pet dogs
is intelligent and gregarious
a skilled mimic it can learn to speak
and invariably it makes
a most affectionate and entertaining
pet when domesticated

being a excellent liar

John Larry Krafchenko was indeed a man of striking appearance, with strong, prominent features. He had a large head with thick black hair so thick it would fall in his eyes and a black moustache. His fearless eyes of steel grey, with just a hint of green, that looked out form under heavy dark brows, would remind one of a lynx, if you had ever run acrost that animal. A handsome debonair man, dressed in the latest fashions, he could hold you with those eyes of his whenever he wished to do so. More than once at Flo Williams' he could flash those sparking eyes on the fairer sex he was such a lady-killer. They were girls however who went in for this make-believe "entertainment" but they sure fell for that guy whenever he turned his eyes on them, being a excellent liar and a most persuasive gentlemen.

cunning linguist

perfectly cunnilingual will bring you all sing you all aphorisms & idioms a dictionary of catch phrases pssstt what the catchword catch as catch can before you kick the can snatches of talk talk of snatches specially for the amusement of all you stiff-necked tight-lipped sharp-tongued law-abiding close-mouthed white folks 'd face the muse sick only pay lip service takin a dim view of thumbing yr noses not up to what 's smack-dab in front of you not at all in good taste bound to prick up a few ears raise a few eyebrows you high-brows

upon my word
whats the world coming to

you should come straight to the point
no sense no use beatin bout the bush
beatin the bush
bumming around
or roughing it
in the bush for that matter
that will get you nowhere
cept pie-eyed & bushy tailed
make you all bushed out is what it will do
it will put you into a brush with danger
spend your time trying to put out brush fires
itll be the brush off sure as shootin
unless you brush up on
this bush league stuff
youll come within a whisker of
ruining the bushings
gettin all tongue-tied
with her tongue twisters
make a lot of tongues wag you bet

god the snapper on that woman she was sittin on a gold mine ha–ay clementine over here yr sittin on a gold mine hear tell i told her she was corrupting minors she interjected miners yr goddamn tootin this heres a mine field & me im layin charges i replied

    I too am a safe cracker she wld say at times like these. wheww the snap decisions shed force you into / shed make without any input from me Make it snappy Snap to it those kind of things Get a move on slowpoke How are you ever going to get ahead, you don't put in for it? she was thinking only of me she sd as her lips parted count me in i wanna enter where ya get the entry forms Snap it up will ya sugar she alwaz sd ginger sd just snapping at you all the time the little sweetie till yd think shed snapped what a pain in the neck don hafta snap my head off do you angela

    you know the kind
    shed whine & moan
    wouldnt let things slide
    in her unseemly haste
    Hold your tongue
    Bite your tongue
    You young whipper snapper
    You bush whacker you
    but her shed raise blisters on your uncle dick
    shed come so quick that or
    yd lose yr tongue
    in a cold snap
    well howd you like to get caught in a cold snap
    sufferin from frost bite
    yeah got nother thot comin now

    well look i was way out on a limb for her only chance i had was to snap out of it before it was too late geez what a hot tempter always snapping at a guy. You are a fine one to talk, she sd. Filling me with hot air. alls i was tryin was to get ahead with that woman willin to take the plunge oh sure i knew id be in way over my head to begin with i knew that but i was willing to pull out all the stops an organ pumping away full tilt ahead that sort of thing geez i cld have taken a header easy as not of course i was trying to save my own neck i admit that but i still dont know what come over me lipping off at her like that just when i thot i had an in but she wouldnt give me much as a smell wld you believe that woman don she know oral sex is in & she an inn keeper too shld be takin in lodgers

well i was desperate lookin for a way in

maybe that is stretching the point just a little but you know how full of quaint & endearin phrases i am an old sweet-talker like me dedicated to a fault. He was a real smoothie all right, I'll grant you that, she asided. oh i got my faults im not perfect hair-line fractures for one thing but i always say why shld i who am i to find fault andrea's or anyone elses for that matter true she needs a little touchin up st iches & i wld actually like to get the goods on her & you know something just gimme my head coz im a real cracker jack at the crack of dawn if i do say so myself well blow me down it never dawned on me eh till now like i was saying ill work it in somehow longs i got a decent head start

    'mere a sec
    always good tip you young fellas should know
    give them an inch & they'll
    make a smile
    stick with me boys
    i got an in
    always good to meet'm head on
    be up front with it
    there are those who hold with a glancing blow
    but whatever position you take
    never get side-tracked i always say
    never fail you always head off trouble that way
    or you wldnt get a word in edgewise
    Funny position to be in, is it not? she sd.
    Perhaps it will give you a slanted view?
    nah gettin a little on the side 'so.k.
    Oh John, how could you? How could you be so inclined?

well first thing's to eyeball up the situation
heads up play is what's needed

tip top top notch i say
& then in the same breath
out stoppin to catch the breath
get in good with them right off the bat
out battin an eyelash man
lemme give you a tip honey you say for starters
here's what you do
what you say for openers
to get things cracking
this could crack things wide open

only fair to warn them tho don get caught in the draft
& be respectful beholden look up to them they like that
but above all no sense losin yr head

so wha's up i sd
Search me she sd
& so i did having a searching
mind & a quick tongue
Look, John. she sd
'm lookin 'm lookin
I could show you a thing or two, she sd.
show me show me
Fine, we will get the show under way.
come on id say
off & on that is
you cant repeat yrself too often
& besides i was counting on her instincts
heads i win tails she does too

Go ahead she said
i cld see she was a cream
puff a push over
a soft touch quick
on the uptake
Drop in some time why don't you handsome?
she was havin me on
& then some
to top off everything
she was putting me on
tighter than a safety belt
I can't quite place you sailor, she sd. Sorry.
well les take off to points unknown
i was getting under his skin you could tell
but it was no skin off my nose
things would work out in the end

Kessa

sssskkk sskk sskk here pussy pussy come on come on Kessa
oh what a pretty pussy yes you are you are so pretty sure
sure you are yes such a pretty pussy so pretty

come on Kessa

come on over here come to me come to see me come here come
on pussycat oh she is so dainty yes she is so pretty so yes
such a nice pussy arent you Kessa come on come here come on
there there theres such a nice pussy so nice there yes she is
she is so nice so pretty mmhhmmm oh so nice so nice and warm
Kessa my she is yes such a nice pussy so warm

like that eh pussycat like that dont you
you like that yes like
that

   eyes close and
open & green they are green
green shining and warm
& singing shaking
(inside) your singing shaking
your singing inside
  &

                         my arm
      blood
my arm pricked
blood bright
red blood on my
                    arm

March 22, 1984

Dear Editor,

I for one am not in the least amused by Dennis Cooley's writings. And I know from talking to others that they have had it up to here with all this filthy language. How can any person, any sensitive person, bring themselves to utter such disgusting words? Much less think of them in the first place. There are perfectly good words available, why doesn't the author use them, or is he only trying to boost sales or like a little boy rub our noses in those things he isn't mature enough to deal with himself.

The words are bad enough but every time I reread those passages I find more and more obscenity shoved down my throat. Sex everywhere. It is crawling with sex. It is as if the author is obsessed and can not let go. Or he may be on dope. And they call this poetry. Where do we find these tasteless things in the classics, why did not Homer and Shakespeare do it if its so "necessary" to "art"?

I understand that Mr. Cooley is a professor at the University. Well, I should like to suggest that those who are offended as I am by this perverted permissiveness should have him fired from so important a position. Perhaps he has no respect for him self, but can he have any real respect for his students either then. I can just see him now sneering and laughing at any sign of human goodness in his class, holding young people with fear of God or considerations up to ridicule. And the tax prayers good hardworking people like my husband and I, are paying for this. I do not want to censor the honest and valued work of deadicated professors, there are lots of them surely, but I cannot in good conscience sit back and say nothing in a case like this one now. Surely they should not permit cynical atheist attacks on what has made Canada what it is today.

I can only shudder to think what resentments this man is nursing and what bitterness he is instilling in susceptible young minds. I wouldn't in the lest be surprised if he votes NDP.

I wish I could forgive him, but he has betrayed his position of trust.

Yours sincerely,
(MRS.) Agnes Klassen

**last will & test
i meant**

        i am
john krafchenko
        i john saw
& said
              they said
                    i can tell you
    they said
        i am
      i was
a wan & a wan
    ted man
i was not wise

    they wanted
        to say
i wanted
        to tell you

      i won
dered what
    they meant
instead
    i have
told you
    what I saw
& said

            i have   grown
            sick with your
            penny   pinching ways

            penny is perennial
            riches   for ever

i am   always
         coming
back   to her
missing her
crooked smile

the crow case

pulling our bodies down the side
walk pulling our bodies down
the sidewalk   May 24
one bitch of a spring   so cold
airs puckered   like a bulls ass in flytime
& not a robin in sight

Ken Hughes & I   were kids
wagons on a string of beer
on our way   to the student pub
we are   walking for our daily bread

aaw **AWW**   over head
christ   hes moved into town now
a clear case of life imitating art
a nest of pick-up sticks
& crow   I swear   leans
way over   /he wants
to tell me some
thing / & damn well
    winks at me
      knowingly
  just like that
right out loud

    right beside St. John's
     this was
  I swear
it was
    first thing you know
   hell be *cooley cooley* rapping
     at my window   telling me how
to write   over night hes   a goddamn critic
     first chance he gets

PINS FROM SHIRT WERE USED ON LOCK

How Krafchenko got into the photographer's room at the police station, in effecting his escape from the place over a week ago, has been solved. It seems that Percy Hagel brought the captive a new shirt one day, which had not yet been undone, it having three small pins in it at the time. Krafchenko took the pins, preserved them carefully and when the time came, picked the lock on the door of the photograph room successfully. He had been an expert locksmith, and he remarked to Buxton, it was told yesterday, that it had been an easy task for him to open the door. It opened the first time he picked at the ball tumblers, he said. In some manner he had ascertained that the lock was of this kind, that it could be opened by forcing up all three of the ball tumblers contained therein.

freeze up

                      a few pebbles of
        rain red dust & the
creak of hinges   working hard   & dark cracks
    open   cranks its shutters   open & will
          not close for the night

                under the streetlights
                dark drinks the light
                you can see its breath
                horses at lightpoles
                stamping like ghosts

over night frost soaked in railway tracks
chains of it jangle gardens
tangle the tomatoes in steel

      inside night
vertebrae hang from out neck
on wires of winter

am a tingle in dawn now
taps on your window
panes on the blankets
a bleeding of white
where you have lain

frost in morning snaps on
electric in dawn

when dark drank the light
from your hand

gypsophila

                                        now
                        the new snow brightens
            my window deepens
                                    lays it light
upon the ground
                    the grass below
                                holds it grassgreen
                into the yellow warmth
                                        in early November
                seeds tighten/flare
                        under this skin of
                            snow singing
        a billion glass suns
                            in the night
) remembering
    Penny Lyn
                    her gypsophila
                                in our garden
                puffs of gypsophila
                                    white vapour
                                            blown
                        around the orange
                burn of marigolds

in August the ochre
ate its way
scalding thru the
window of my room
& you bathd/breathd in
the slick white acid
inside untoucht
that moment
cool & still
inside the bed

                                        here
                        in the mellow spill
                                    of sunfall
                the wax spaces
                        tell me
you are gone
Nov 8
        your letter says
                        Toronto
                out of the tinbarn box clicks
) the winter dreaming
                at my door
        the words that have not come
                dont take my words love lightly
                        your voice tells
                                of the quick
        cells rising
                    flicker
cells your body carries
                        growing
                                        dividing &
                                            growing
                        growing & dividing
us now
you now
                these 2000 miles
                            a child's breath away

skunked

                well yr scrabblin out
       past scrub oak
          judo choppin yr way thru the black
black as suknaskis canning pot
              splattered with stars
          night's thickern arnason's coffee after
a saturday night drunk
squirrels you got the drop on them dont let out a peep
       you (& them) crabbin over scrappy no-name bushes
             chunks of clay

        couple baby crows
             still gurglin round the outhouse
     kids in the pool hall
           the old lady this morning
                not able to shove
enuff frogs & horse buns into
                    those hoppers
     to keep them shut

       spades   pails   rope
all jump up in front of you
        & the spruce sprayin
   resin juice like a crack
           regiment of noname winter tomcats
    fortified with fire hoses
onto the air sweeter than cin
    namon &
          at last there
             you are the living
   rooms pissyellow
chamberpotted out
      onto the ground

                    yr eyes dipped full of
                        kitchen yellow
    it scribbles out like a wink
                            the yellow

    and yr on home ground now
                    stinko on rye &
        you gotta take a leak so bad yr
                    back molars are floatin

    its a bladder dash from here on in
     mosquitoes vicious as a million laws the minions of
         & fishflies elbowin to be first into the spider webs
                its a frantic mid-summer madness

                        but at last you are there
                    it is you & Timothy E
                        in the dark
                        one on one
                        he has his use

                            so—oooo
                    you let er go

    you drain the crank case &
            yr about to
         minuet back to
           the blackjack table andys waitin
                    that very minute
               like a sleepy raccoon with his beer
                                        when

wwwhhh

        death blows up yr pantleg

there she is this
        amblin footloose from the chicken coop
      mamma skunk caboosing
                    6 more
  winsome as the mayor's wife
                   herself
right beneath yr nose
        feathers on her breath
              & blood

  blood in her eye

Criminal Life

A Compleet, Unxpurgate, & a Dull
terated Hystori of the Knee Fairious
Loveys & the Fureeus &
Vrius Robries of the Moste No

torias BLOODiE JaCQUA Free

quentre of Bars and Brathls,
Fami liear of Wenches in Wynepeg, & All of Man
nyere of Lewde Low Lifes, Weere In
HIs Most Sekret & Bar berus
Endyes, Hys Outrages Hole-ups, his Mons
terus Breakeyings
& Aynt ryngs, & His Mosty Unherd Of Safe Krakings are Ahl
Set in *Tree Lytle* & Iks
Posd to Fulle Publicke Vuw,
For the Comeon Benefye & the Up
Lyftyng Edi facshuns of
MEmBUrSe of the SpIECiES ———
who Myte Therein Bee Pro Teckted
from His moste Abaminabl Trics, Lyes, Jestus, Ruzes,
Cheetes, Guyzes, Stane-Ins,
Hair razying & Sudititisush
Sedushuns & Othere of Scapaids Tew
Numros to Mentyne.

she sd

        when you die she sd
              she sd
     its like
ghosts
   shucked off
       the white
  flesh in your teeth
the bones melt
    in your mouth

           she sd
              look
     its zippered
 silk
    shucked off
she sd
     the white teeth
  sweat in the flesh
   the wet seeds
        sweet (as
   salt) in my mouth melt

           when you die
  she sd

vulva jig

                                                                      well

                                         take a swig

                     riggedy jig & a
          way we go

    o vulva oooo
    when i blew
    in on you
    we were over
    due i was over
    joy over you
    i don't think
    i ever will be
    over you
    & we were over
    joyed & me i was dew
    E-eyed id say
    & you you took me on
    my own say so
    you took me in
    id says its so
    & oh it is touch & go
    to live with/in sight
                              of you

                  & now you
are takin me for a ride
in yr vulva you
        till yur good
and thru with
        me and me id

got the inside track
with my slide trombone
    oh the bone to find
        the bone a part
             a part to find
      to find the part
                my heart is ready
              o my heart is needy is reedy to

  play the parts
 a fiend to find
 a bone a part
      a part of you
 o dont depart

                theres
            a bone to find
            a bone
                to find my
      self confined in you
      id confide in you

     bone of you
     to pick with you
     till im
         bone sore with you
         bon soir to you
         but still in all
         in luv with you
         id queue up for you
         tdz what id do
         fine to be
         confined in you
         tdz mighty kind of you

                    still / i pined for you
                    pained with you
                    lost my mind in you
                    blind by you
                    still in all i
               like the view
     if it comes to that

                                        entre nous
                                        m'lady ma chère
                                        i wld woo
                                        you / vous
                                        bill & coo for you
                                        right now avow to you
                                        blow vowels for you

& its true
cant do with
out you too
what wld i do in
lieu of you
be thru with you
outside of you
without a clue
if you withdrew

               but im all in too
               in sight of you
               in side of you
               beside my
               self do

                        u know that 2
                                        & u
                        got what it takes
                        luvly liquid
                        uv ulu

          epi glottal
          oughta coddle
          taught all the
          clitoral choral
          neither nor all
          the clit
          oral tra
          dition the
          sedition of our ways
          or all glottal
          not at all
          a verse
          to poly
          glottal perverse

                        o u
                        my luvly liquid u
                        u liquid friction
                        sat is
                        faction
                        it is no fiction
                        faction free

o my dear
can you not find it
within you
can you fit me

in im full of sin
cerity charity too
& you in alacrity
buttering my heart
the very heart uv yuh
the way yuh muv
i fully approve
wld like to groove
o prove 2 u
uvula
my luv uv ya
uncover my deep
deep luv
my luv of ya
    uvula
    uvula
lovely glug uv ya
    uvula

wherein & whereupon im
so invulved with yuh
revolved round yuh
dissolved in yuh
volubly vulvubly vulgarily
in the peoples voice
luvin ya vulva
the way yuhve evolved
luvin ya
so cant let ya go
    dont
let me go
just hold me
tight & dont
     let go

say it isnt so
        uvula
it isnt
    is it
time to visit
        uvula
    is it
        vulva

be dull without ya
if yull nullify me
lulla by me
one hulla bah loo
if you get sore on me
even the score with me

        but when i blows on u
        i can c
        that u r
        soft on me
        velour vulva
        way u go soft on me
        way 2 go
        it doesnt show

        always good to see you tho
        tho you don't always glow
        when you see me grow &

        coming so &
        so
        im good to you
        good 4 u
        freud knew

      tho i feud with u
      we two
      we too
      shld be 1
      in the end
      im glued to you
      lewd with you
      renewed in u
      imbued with u
      when im nude with u
      even so
      even odds

      odd i shld say that
      even so

so its so long
bound to be seein yuh
hopin yuhll come round
to seein my way
in the end

      so im
stickin with ya
stuck on you
whats due to you
                      vulva **ooo**
                      coz u r always new
                      & coz you
                            & only u

wont let me
u wont never let me
down
       wont never let me
down in the end

           adieu to you
                              yurs luvingly
                                luving yurs
                                                bloody jack

           & many happy returns

         T.C. Laws   **The jig is up.**

so glad

 just to

      with

   dance

      to

glad

         just

     so

    to

       dance

     with

       just

        you

                                                psychic

                              the hard thread
                                    Fanica
                    over it
                              hand full of tendons
they are yellow
              her crochet
needle hooks & her thumb bones
                       are in my chest pulling
      and pulling
                    tight
                                she is
           twisting
she is twisting
      the red and purple
                    ligaments
           together
inch by inch
                she is
     drawing in
           a bed-spread
                    the limp weight of it
           drowning the mouth and nose
                                up and over
                    the broken parts
knitting
       together
              knotting
       shut

me a linen doily in her hands

they leave their traces

        every spring
our back yard throws up new wonders
old wire stones of all sizes nails hundreds of nails
(mostly bent) a buckle chunks of wood one head from a
sledge hammer a porcelain knob pieces of china some with blue
markings buttons cans that look like theyre eaten by metal moths
hunks of concrete pieces of what looks like black top bolts some
with nuts some without old posts a few coins badly decayed
marbles there are a few marbles bits of brick and crumbled masonry
straps of iron broken most often at the bolt holes something we take
to be animal teeth a spoon with no handle cracked vertebrae

& once a horse shoe leapt like a frog into the air & we put it by the shed
to save lids from tins & jars rivets coloured bottles pieces of rope
wed find unidentifiable bars of metal squirms of wire for chickens
or plaster screws caked with rust a spoon Diane found a spoon one
time

& theres one spot at the top of the garden
where the garden tractor grinds &
grinds on something hard
only it never appears

      we put them in piles
      these strange articles
          every spring
      the leavings of lives dribble
      a litter of nouns
        refuse to speak

once when we first started the garden i pulled some flattened
eavestroughing out some times there are
handles from cups lengths of chain in one corner one
time there was this huge lid for a barrel & we chopped

it out   2 feet deep   Diane & I   with a pick in the mud
we pried it free   & we squashed it as much as we cld
for the garbage

this place they sd once was a blacksmiths
at the head of a ferry where
Riel waited for MacDougall
& theres a sign   just down Pembina
by a pile of rubble
that tells about it

ST. NORBERT
where the Métis stopped the men from the East
where Krafchenko passed on his way to Plum Coulee

                      the garden
always wild with sloughings every spring blooming
scabs or whole skins the years have shivered off

one time   it was a chamber pot lid   only it had a screw
sticking through   loosely with no knob   so maybe it was
                      a cooking pot

the odds & ends we pile up each spring
presents in a way   a certain presence
in profusion raining up on us

                    the diggings form a past
                    we move vertically into
                    Krafchenko in vertigo dropped in to
                    with his blacksmith father
                    & his outrageous story
                    & his lonely wife

but for us   the garden
continues to turn over   its miracles
like a carnie in a shell game
this time its a cold day   in a cold spring
                         /May 26
& Im digging our new crop of left overs
Diane dips   dandelions
out of the lawn   with a silver wand   when she kneels
over close to the ground   can she hear what
they say   what they want   the roots & the worms
aligning with forces in the air
& I   I plug carrot & pea seeds   into the ground
where they suck on dirt & wreckage

and all the time gleaning
the annual sprinkle of glass & rocks & nails
once more I rake out the newest finds

    but this time its something   heavier
    lean to pick it the way you   snap beans off
    its squat & scaled
    I have no idea how long its been there
    chemically closed over the years
    but it is there &   I suppose
    it shld be a sign
an old padlock shut up in the ground
)if i hold it to my ear
            or soak it in liquid solvent
            will it   open up
                      transformed
  a poppy in sun
          open cracks in your brain

       write this thinking of Krafchenko
in that blacksmith shop   thinking of him
in that jail   waiting to break out
                       of his silence
letters in the law archives
their fountain-pen spillage

imagine him   on the road past our place
      driving shear across
      the empty fields
      where weeds fill in

trying to pick   secrets out of the furrows
in my mind   he a picker
of locks & pockets   of lockets & plackets

                     me a sort of verb
                                  writing this
                out
                        trying to set things
                                      right

god with his yellow teeth

        their glitter
you do not care for
    no/
        nor
  their eyes bulge to brass purse
      snaps before they bust
open

        god hunched
    under shingles of
            blood

    god leans
heavy & sweating on his hoe
        then (curious)
            kneels
  stiff in his coveralls
        sniffing
way over like he cant see
      peering his eyes are
  smeared with mucous
        & exploded stomachs
    shreds of lungs
   spatter his beard
      cores from a ruptured boil
  & once / chicken blood sputtered on Ivans snow
          sprinkles
    on his shirt too

gods sleeves rolled up
the guts stuck to his squashed nostrils
     god snuffing & puttering
             in the dirt

   his breath. when he breathes.
          in his mouth
     the smell of overnight cheese

remember
     saw that in the toilet once
  live snot epileptic

god squats
    fastidious as a plastic surgeon
picking strings of red phlegm
    from his beard off the ground
        their snail brains perfectly
           poached in the shells
    god is snapping
  rib bones in his jaws
       precise as a dog
god with his yellow teeth
  is biting the last bits out
  from under his broken nails
      intent as an infant
    monkey nibbling
        on bugs & scabs
  fat and of an agreeable taste

a curious
        epicure god sipping
    our blood swished
thoughtfully in his mouth
          for balance & bouquet
   spits & pisses
wipes the grease on his pantleg
then he chops up the left-overs
         puffing as he works
             them like potato peels
     steadily/   into the earth

all in all a wonderful hoe-down
& he saw it & said
        he said it was
   good
did not he say so himself/
                       god

       & in yr head trickle too
       boxcars full of timebombs
       tickles of bugs
       down on their luck
       in frantic buzzes
       making tracks across the coal
       before / tricked/
                 one by one
          flipping
            they snuff in beautiful tacks of fire
                         jelly arcs
               from yr glass
                       eye cut

       tiddly winks
                    flipping out

a truck of blood in the eye of god
the eye of god
           ticking

jail break, update

We can't yet tell where it all started but there were some early signs. Days ago inmates began to approach The Grammarians about their complaints, with little effect, it has been reported. Apparently they weren't listening. Warden Morris, who declined to be interviewed, is reported to have favoured life sentences for those that have now slipped away into the prairie vernacular. He expressed deep consternation about the lessening of standards and violations of protocol, wondering whether cooley might be involved in the assaults on erudition and good taste.

Authorities are not sure how the convicts were able to evade the tight security, but, as I say, Peter, the guessing is that they were disguised in lower cases and, in some instances, anonymity. They were then able, on pretext of making their way to chapel, to sneak past a check point virtually undetected when the brackets failed to hold. And then, further down in the sentence, they managed to slip through a comma fault almost unimpeded.

That's when they made a dash for the library. It was then that the infinitives split and the lines make a clean break for it.

The situation sounds serious, Walter. What we are hearing here, in Eastern Canada, this out of York University, is disturbing. Frankly, it is being said that local prairie poets, scarcely known outside of Manitoba, have been cultivating a nostalgia for boyhood innocence and a naïve belief in orality.

That's one view, Peter, though there is one other theory. It has it that the prisoners got out by hiding inside an obscure book of poetry that Guards scarcely noticed. Book Reviewer has informed police that Leslie Vermeer, under cover as a University of Alberta Press agent, had smuggled Bloody Jack into the reading room and, when Librarian was distracted, left with the whole kit and caboodle under her arm, cleaned out every last one of the criminal elements and took them with her, a whole series of shocking prepositions, vowing to give BJ a new hearing.

How is it possible that Oral Poems could so easily have escaped notice, Walter?

Well, this theory, doubtful though it appears at first blush, seems corroborated by the text itself, as Dr. David Arnason, he of the Litote, has assured us in exclusive interview from his cottage in Gimli. "Bloody Jack," he has told CBC, "is set entirely in sans serif and is, as a matter of fact, housing a massive number of Calligraphics, Cooley among them." According to Arnason, he had himself rounded up the text, years ago, excised as much as possible, did what he could to put it in some kind of order, and brought it to public light. This latest outbreak, he said, baffled and stunned him. He has no idea, he said, what to make of this. He did say, however, that the ampersands had probably coordinated the whole affair and that, though he was normally fond of them himself, he thought in this case they would have a lot to answer for—the ampersands and the dangling prepositions, it was hard to know which was worse.

And where does that leave us now, in the spring of 2002?

Police are now looking for an overweight book, Bloody Jack, in his late teens, long black hair, and wearing a University of Alberta cover. It is not certain at this point, but the escapee, now that he is at large, may well have with him a dust jacket he will slip on or off as it suits him. He has been known to introduce himself as a wanted man and, under the smallest provocation, will not hesitate to use the puns with which he is armed. Book himself is suspected of harbouring Wanted Men and Unwanted Poems.

Reader suspects that Bloody Jack is in hiding somewhere with Seed Catalogue and Billy the Kid, though it is hard to confirm this report, Catalogue and Kid being reluctant to admit knowing the criminal. It is feared, even more likely, bj may try to contact Headframe or Marsh Burning, known and dangerous associates, who have been seen to frequent a shady establishment, bp, aka Boson Pizza, at 2729 Pembina. It was there the suspects are known to have entered into their nefarious conspiracies, their breathings together.

If you know of Book's whereabouts, you are asked to contact Sergeant Barker Pen at Crime Stoppers. You need not reveal your name and your call will not be traced. Informants are warned nevertheless to be careful, for it is likely, according to inside sources, that Publisher has threatened to take Book Reviewer hostage, and, if need be, Critic.

It is a strategy that might well backfire, however, if Critic is willing, as some suspect he is, to sacrifice Book Reviewer in the interests of an early apprehension. Meanwhile Book Seller waits.

data

I have not the exact data to hand for Manitoba, but here they are for Ontario: During the year 1907, according to the official Government returns, it cost Ontario $314,315.03 for the maintenance of criminal and mentally affected immigrants imported into the province by the Dominion Government's Immigration Department, as follows:

1,517 patients in hospitals for the insane	$227,550.00
4,314 prisoners in jail	61,339.23
289 prisoners in central prisons	25,425.80
Total	$414,315.03

This bill, large as it appears, for punishing crime among foreigners, does not stand still. It grows in Ontario and every other province every year. But taking Ontario at the 1907 figure for all the following years to 1919, it has cost that province $4,771,780.36 to nurse and punish the class of foreigners that was thrust upon her.

Johnny got a lickin

Johnny over the ocean
Johnny over the sea
Johnny broke a beer bottle
Blamed it on me

I told ma
and ma told pa
and Johnny got a lickin
Ha ha ha

How many lickings did he get?
    1
    2
    3
    4
    5
    6
    7
        all good children go to

  hell & back
   back
   back

Jack's dictionary of cunning linguists

novitiate: a johnny come lately
rabid: foaming at the mouth
aging: can't afford to lose face / agen
despondent: is sunk in depression
effete: a poet taster, nosegay some would have it
swinging: lets down his hair
puritanical: her lips are sealed
conscientious: gives 'm a fair shake
tonsorial: gets in the hair
impetuous: dives in head-first
indifferent: gives the cold shoulder
radical: in a hot bed of activity
reckless: headed for a crackup
hard-up: has trouble making ends meet
bilingual: is beside herself, he speaks with a forked tongue
turbulent: is often feeling floosie
disapproving: favours a crackdown
outstanding: is head and shoulders above
myopic: can't see beyond his nose
meek: turns the other cheek
loyal: sticks it out through thick & thin
bankrupt: goes belly up
clumsy: hits it right on the nose
marginal: involved in split decisions
timid: won't find fault with anyone
hermaphroditic: really comes into herhishisher own
inquisitive: an eager beaver
thorough: doesn't want to leave anything out
lesbian: speaks in the mother tongue
sentimental: lives in nether nether land
optimistic: believes s/he is making head way
sadistic: always beats it
moralistic: makes snap judgements
reformed: gets a weight off herhis shoulders

journalistic: gives a blow by blow account
inexperienced: fuzzy faced
parsimonious: speaks with pursed lips the tightwad
truculent: holds her/his own
proletarian / fallen / cursed: lives by the sweat of his brow
divine: she brings down the world on his head
experienced: fuzzy faced
fed up: will tell him/her where to get off
tempted: within an inch of his wife
angry: cuts off his nose to spite his face
lucky: experiences a windfall
promiscuous: has a loose tongue
          likes a loose tongue too
malcontented: airs grievances
impatient: plays hard and fast
hypocritical: is two-faced
epicurean: develops a taste for it
enterprising: 'd snap you up in a minute, a split second
inventive: eager to find a new wrinkle, vents her views
witty: a real wag with women
speculative: gets caught in boom & bust
aboriginal: is leary of pale faces
investigative: an undercover agent
          fears someone will blow her cover
sadomasochistic: deals is dealt a heavy blow
          catches you in one hell of a tongue-twister
acrobatic: goes into a nose dive
          a tail spin
English: keeps a stiff upper lip
equivocal: faces a split decision
aggressive: knows you can never get off easy
duplicitous: between a lick and a promise
Freudian: trusts in a slip of the tongue
harried: sometimes s/he's all in

competitive: busy nosing out rivals
snotty: looks down his nose at
narcissistic: the spitting image
lucky: wins by a nose
despondent: down in the mouth
correspondent: keeps in touch
premature: finds things are touch and go
impatient: always beats it
traditional: is above that sort of thing
reserved: makes no bones about it
      will tell him/her where to get off
athletic: calling audibles in the huddle (jocular asides)
      sure sure i have a glib & fluid tongue so do you you
      too for my part i am voluble [fr. *volvere* to roll;
      akin to oe wealwian to roll, Gk *eilyein* to roll, wrap]
      hence a rolling tongue & yr rollin over wrapt as in
      vulva [integument, womb; akin to Skt ulva womb, L
      vol-vere to roll—more at VOLUBLE] to speak up, to pipe
      up a pipe dream, blowing bubbles & she is forever
      blowing me, to roll yr r's my bonnie lass; to babble on
religious: wholly committed
devout: holy thine
macho: hard nosed
offensive: rubs people the wrong way
rude: can't keep a civil tongue in his head
humbled: faces a real come down
improvident: up to the chin in
fickle: blows hot and cold
casual: comes breezing in at the last moment
uncoordinated: way out of whack
disadvantaged: is really up against it
unskilled: a fringe player
venturesome: lets down the hair
over bearing: baring down on him

rabid: foaming at the mouth fomenting trouble
confused: doesn't know what's eating her
fierce: shed box his ears
legalistic: issues sub poenas
opportunistic: johnny on the spot
            blows his chances
athletic: breezes thru the warm ups / the preliminaries
exploitive: plays you for a sucker
Catholic: gets into bad habits
jocular: does laps to stay in shape
            lip/lap lip/lap lip/lap
French: wins by default
            :
vain:
            ::

            : really lays one on you

            : two faced

disloyal: does an about face

    : lays it on a little thick
    : sticks with you through thick & thin

I M : U :: U R : B

he thinks of her

boats yes quick
silver sailboats
once on Lake Winnipeg
boats & you like
wet fingernails wet
on the lake
vapour

                        & hair smell of you wet
                        in crash of night tar
                        throating of you
                        stay with me
                        stay with me
                        & red rain on me
                        crushed cartilage
                        in the frozen rain

after the dance

        poplars gulping
        june shouting with love &
        night beer giggling
        undresses day
        moves through me in a slur
        my swim suit sticky from
        the lake under my dress
        where we go in the dark
        les go skinny dipping hhnn
        voice in throats the chuu—unk
        when they close a car door
        moon slides off is a slip
        from the hip of night
        leaves tight with blood & he
        squashing wind out of mosquitoes

        he close with sweat
        sweet on my breasts my
        nipples his spit is
        moon is a cinnamon
        candy in my mouth now
        the slippery roller
        coaster of him wanting
        those dark brown eyes
        where the light goes
        funny

when light dumps out of the trianon
jumps onto the ground
& the sax shakes out
in the trees come
back blue lady come back
falls on smell of sunburn & grass
cold cream & sand

around us like yes water we are
driving the night smells & you
dont care your windows open
you couldnt dont my god wait & he in
my ear yes wetting his words &

                                              the flutter
                            stutter of moon

   shouting with love & the night—

his muse in the guise of a loonie lady comes to him (& desire full in her face)

pudgy moon
        stuffed with sausages
        and sauerkraut
    nudges
you awake and
        cuddles on your pillow
there she is
        wide-eyed & glowing
thats her
        faintly puffing
        & smelling of beer
this crazy woman
she has climbed through the window
        when
(a) your back was turned
(b) she found the ladder
(c) you left it unlatched
(d) your lips are sealed
   you aren't talking, not a word of a lie
shes shoved
        the curtains aside &
there she is now
        rolling her eyes at you
i dont know
        whats got into her
but she seems to have taken a
        shine to me
    the dizzy dame
you'd of thought she would be more serene silene

```
                        so she throws her hair
              across my face
then nuzzles my neck
        and wetlips my ear
        & she so pleased
                moving down over you
        so importunate
        she wont let you go
                how unfortunate
        back to sleep
                        she beaming & beaming
with love at you
```

the end of the line

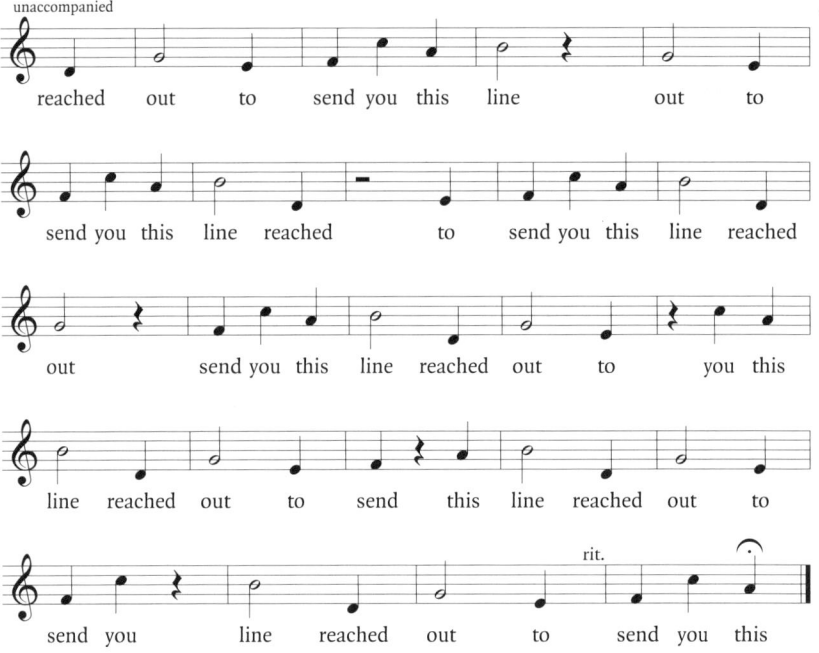

making up

you just made that up
yes you did didn't you did too
coz you cldnt make it in the real world
yr tryn make it in here aincha
I know yr kind
kind of stupid & twice as vain
you cant make it
with the chicks
so yr trying to string em a line
makes no sense to me

so you make it
convincing as you can
such nonsense
          such making
believe

               making it
  up
                   yup
              making it up
                    im making it
    up
          all right
              its hard
                  making
     it up
                   up &
          making
              it
                  making
                         up
   yup
  getting up

```
pity
        making
                just bare
          ly mak
                   ing
   it
                (up)
```

hes got to go down some time

This might interest you. When they were excavating the old Law Courts buildings they didn't have any way of knowing this but where they were digging they ran into the old tunnel. It had been blanked off. They used to lead the prisoners down the tunnel on the way to execution. You might use this: he's got to go down to Hades some time.

                shade of sorrow

Oh yes, actually in that tunnel they'd found the underground pathway through which the prisoners from the condemned cells were taken to their place of hanging. And they didn't know of it on—what do you call those things? the design?

Blueprints?

Well they didn't have any blueprints, there were no blueprints. This thing had just been walled off and forgotten about.

It cost them quite a bit of money in fact, this new building just had to make allowances and stop production.

So what did they do with the tunnel?

They came to terms with it.
But anyway, there it was.
And Tony Tascona told me this
because Tony had been involved in doing that commission.
Yeah.

Is that it?

weather tis nobler

What kind of weather is it (out) to-day?
It is very fine weather.
It is pleasant weather.
It is glorious weather.
It is neither too cold, nor too warm.
The weather could not be finer.
The sky is clear.
Songs drop into birds.
The sun is shining brightly.
We shall have a fine day.
The wind is north (west, south).
The wind is (blows) from the east.
It is too fine to last long.
The weather will soon change.
See, how it is raining!
It is raining very hard.
The rain drops are seeds of wheat.
It is pouring.
It is thundering and lightning.
We shall have a thunderstorm soon.
The clouds are black as used motor oil.
The wind is getting up.
It splashes in my face.
It might blow the goose-bumps off of a hippopotamus.
It is beginning to hail.
The lightning has struck.
It is warm.
It is very hot.
It is sultry.
The sun is smirking.
It is snorting.
It is very dusty.
It is cloudy.
The sky is overcast.

It is cast over us.
It will soon clear up.
Do you see the rainbow?
The storm has stopped talking.
The sun is beginning to grin again.
We shall have a pleasant evening.
It is bracing and cool.
It is a frog.
The days are growing shorter.
The nights are already dry apples.
It is foggy.
We had a heavy fog this morning.
Winter should be dropping around.
It is cold.
A snuffle of cold.
It is freezing.
Winter has arthritis in her knees.
There will be frost to-night.
It will sit on us.
It has tinsnipped the sky.
Do you see the ice on the eaves-troughs?
There has been frost.
How it is snowing!
The snow is barging down in large flakes.
There will be fine sleighing.
I am shivering with cold.
This is a time of shivaree and chivalry.
Surely you know that.
The pond is covered with thick ice.
Let us skate a little.
I have no skates.
I can lend you a pair.
The snow melts (is melting).
It is beginning to thaw.

The cold is starting to wake up.
Do you see these icicles?
They look like knuckles.
The air is loosening.
It will soon be spring.
Pretty soon spring will make smells.
It is a wonderful night.
Night tramps on us.
It is moonlight.
It is starlight.
It is full-moon.
It is new-moon.
It is the first quarter.
It is the last quarter.
The sun is rising.
The sun is setting.
Night will step on us.
Smeared with desire.

in the morning sun
will burn off the birds

with glad gonads grinning

when in brief April the fierce fire-button   first bursts *whoosh*
fighting open a big orange   butterfly burnt
when the Red river roused   roughly carouses
past the curbs collapsing   partitions of cold

then the beer-guzzling   the belle-nuzzling
the cabined and accordioned   the comatose Krafchenko
having in chortles heard   the ding-dong cortisone
and yes he horny having   heeded the chuckle and come-on
heard oestrus erupting erratically   the horse fly frenzy of hers
felt flick of flash   firm flash of flesh
he jigs and he mazurkas   he jumps over the moon
in sight of bums that bloom   a breeze that bobs that boobs
Jack right ready to give up   a grim life of grime
when the west wind   warbles wet with water
coaxes cold and croup   out of laundry on the line
when washed slips and shirts   soak up socks of sun
then Jack brushed dizzy with   sweet whiskey breath

oh then he arises to the go-signs   abrupt as a light switch
Jack the gay girl-grabber   Jack the lusty lass-lover
humps headlong into the green house   he randy rushes
all the grand gonads   glorying and grinning
growing too in their glad handing   the girl gland handling

so brash into the bawling   the brawling barefoot bronze
the raunchy Krafchenko crashes alas   a rutting rooster resigned

the warden

    his breath stretches
                             out stiff in wind
          when he walks
       his breath unwrapping
                     the ribbon candy
      curl in it
snaps out
         like a flag
            in the yard

                    & bacon &
          eggs waiting
      coffee at home
        hot coffee & the kids
          he started it
                 sticky fingers
        over toast

                warden wading
        in muddle of sun
   the puddles of my mind

south thru morris

not a sign of a grader
where the hell those sons a bitches go
when you need them
stinks like burned toast under the dash
kid & Collie rounding up 30 or 40 Holsteins
haystacks melted like rocks out of the snow
& we blown blank as stone
on the skim of snow

dirty as Laws very own snot sleeve
flakes big as cigarette papers then
last February & the horses jumpin over
drifts like jack rabbits

here in April miles of furrows vacant show
the cold bumping thru
floorboards slowing in the legs slows
                more & more
           the drones graze
& the car choking on rusted plugs
Lord forgive us our manifold sins

cold into the joints auguring like grain
Gardiner in the back gazes like a pig
jiggling sits on the giggling
in all his knees & elbows smart
Alec Gardiner *hey watch it buddy* giggling

chug south thru Morris south
            then west 4
hours to Plum Coulee
brake sharp AAARR$_{RUUUU}$GGGGGHHHHHA
aaaruughha   across the tracks shaking

Karen Long reminiscing

Oh, you know, I guess I would say he was, oh, sinister in some way. Well, maybe not sinister, exactly. I mean he wasn't mean or cruel or getting into trouble the way some of the others were. I guess what I'm trying to say is how odd he was, he wasn't really like the other kids, really. I guess that's not surprising.

You know he grew up under some pretty difficult conditions? His mother and father never knew very much English and I guess you could say didn't have any great standing in the community. They grew up—you're going to laugh at this, but it's true—they were raised in a tar paper shack over there by the tracks. It's gone now, been gone for 40, 50 years, but there was this tar paper shack used to stand over by the Adamsons'. I could take you over there, show you right where it used to stand. Well, that's where he grew up, anyway. I know it sounds like an old story, doesn't it? But he did, he actually lived in a tar paper shack when he was growing up.

No. He never did much in the way of reading and writing in those days. Not that you could tell, anyways. He was smart as a whip, knew all kinds of languages and later, I hear, was even a writer. But he hated school and got into terrible rages at the teacher. Never really joined anything, neither, went his own way and other people just, well, came to him somehow is what they did. If anyone ever did. You can check for yourself.

So that's what I was getting at when I said just now he was sinister. He seemed to have some terrible fascination for people. That's the thing I remember most about John Krafchenko was how he pretty much went his own way. Maybe he had work to do, I don't know, but you never saw much of him, whatever it was. After school the other kids would hang around a bit, you know kids, they like to keep things just to themselves from adults. We would traipse home slow as could be cause there were chores and so we poked around at the slough, that sort of thing.

That's right. And it was a good chance to see your friends. But Jack could hardly bear it. It wasn't really because the other kids didn't like him, either, or that he wasn't even popular in a way, he never seemed to fit in, quite.

That, plus our parents. They were a little concerned. I suppose they were right. But it never seemed so at the time. You know how they'd never come right out and say so, but you could tell. There'd be little hints. We should watch out and we wouldn't want to disappoint ourselves, would we? That kind of thing.

Even so, there was always something kind of special about him somehow. You never could quite figure him out—not that we worried a lot about it, or him—but you kind of always wondered what's going on in his head. And I guess when he grew up he led quite the life, didn't he? So, whatever it was those days took him away on his own, caught our eye, well I guess, I guess in the end it came out in some unfortunate ways.

But you know, when he got just a little bit older, when the rest of us got a little older this was, quite a few of the girls were watching out for him. You could almost see it coming. Not that they were frightened of him, that's not what I mean. It was more a matter of that they were quite … well, they were quite attracted to him I guess you would have to say. Ask Mrs. Ens, yes Erica Ens, the redhead, that's her, she'll tell you. I could tell you a thing or two about those times. Her too. Just ask her.

Well, no, he didn't do much at school, John, or go in for going to dances like some of the young boys around, playing in bands, that sort of thing. Still, he was always popular, I guess popular, you would say. I don't know quite how to put a finger on this, he seemed to have some kind of excitement. And then when he got older, the girls just got more and more interested. Even then, when he would of been oh 12, 13, he had this very special charm. I am sure you know what girls that age are like, a little silly sometimes. And, oh, it's, it's nothing we could ever quite admit to ourselves, then, but we giggled among ourselves, us girls, when we were small when he was walking by. That, or we would tease each other now and again the way kids do when he was around.

Once Linda Turner even called to him. Well, not called, actually. What she really did was she sort of sang this song just loud enough he could hear. "Johnnie from over the ocean." You know that one? "Johnnie from over the sea"? A kid's skipping song. Anyways, she sang this song when he was there. Pretended he wasn't, but he knew. Her mom and dad were pretty religious and didn't want her to get mixed up in anything. But she had a crush on him, you could tell. She was doing that for him. And I just closed my eyes and thought "Oh my god Linda, what if he comes in here? What if he comes into the yard and your mom comes home? Then what?"

But he was always like that, Krafchenko—a certain, certain air about him that affected people funny. And even though it was clear the girls went silly over him—clear to everybody but him it seemed, sometimes then—the boys in town didn't mind him either. Funny, isn't it? As a matter of fact, they got along just fine with him, played baseball. Krafchenko was good at that. He was a good athlete. About the best runner in town in those days. You can see for yourself. I remember how in sports days he would always win all the races, never fail. Once he'd been sick but he still did, he was still running and won over all the other boys and was sick to his stomach after. No one ever held that against him, and, like I was saying, the boys never got mad he was so attracted to the girls. He was quite the boy all right.

But I can't tell you much about him, other than that. I don't know about that Dyck thing.

a sign/ some cows

must be getting past lunch
a sign there at the level-crossing
water stiff in ditch
a shack & the tin exhaust
smoking on the roof
4 miles to go
small skeleton of some bird
dangling from the barb wire fence
long johns on the clothes lines
still rigid with night
shredded cattails
& the black&whites lurch
chasing their frost & Gardiner
farts really lets one rip Bell half blind
lays one out laughs & shouting stands pissed
out of his mind in back grins
skinny fist sneezing *looket them go go*
                trips on the words
ya stupid tailpissers go gogogogo
                lady at door agog
                      crashing past in pasture
fastern Monica Playfair at a Sadie Hawkins dance

                      a long time ago

"Subversive Only in a Hyphenated Sense"

—L.A. WYNNE-SMITH
Times Literary Supplement (February 14, 2002)

In this book Cooley is toying with us, if he is not, in fact, merely playing with himself. In the Krafchenko poems we encounter yet another version of extreme modernism, dressed out now in its latest fashion as "post-modern." We are treated, yet again, to a barrage of trivial jokes, to a firebombing of whatever is bizarre or clever. Such raids on the intelligent, and intelligible, shapes of language should no longer be taken seriously. In these verses there is no genuine effort to reach the best in us. There is, rather, an unremitting indulgence in whatever, for the moment, appeals to the author.

How one can be moved by this? What is there to learn? In these poems (Cooley, one gathers, thinks of them as parts of a long poem), what is not obscure is fevered, what is not pretentious is yet careless. Like many of his contemporaries, the author seems convinced that gimmickry can make up for a want of imagination.

Lamentably, one finds no character in this book, no real character that is—one which is fully and causally realized. Instead, we are invited to join in on a casual stream of puns and profanity, all of dubious literary merit. What the author favours—random experience, calculated shock, and sheer buffoonery (offered here as the stuff of the new literature)—in the end can only disappoint. What is wanting is something more human, certainly more humane. Above all, we need writers who speak in full intelligence to the fears and desires of the race.

To be sure, Cooley is not without talent and he does show some promise. In a number of pieces, particularly the love poems, he verges on shot-gun elegance. Perhaps, one day, he could enhance our sense of life. But time and again, not knowing where to draw the line, he loses control of his material or falls into mannerisms. No, this hodge-podge, passed off as "experimental"—some might have said excremental—proves to be one more exercise in vanity. As a result, this material remains, at best, diverting.

It would be sad enough if Cooley were the only offender in this regard. Regrettably, he is not. One fears this book is symptomatic of a larger malaise—a failure of nerve in the Western world. We have, perhaps, lost faith in the terms of a shared life. Evidently we have abandoned hope that the poet can be, as always he has been, a person speaking to others. In the absence of any public language, or of an unalterable standard of excellence, we are left with noise and confusion. We witness, sadly, the contortions of writers eager to leave the tradition behind and unwilling to earn their best work.

We are everywhere beset with such immaturity. One can only hope that, with clear-minded criticism, we can bring a little sense and a greater audience back to literature. To be sure, a little learning is a dangerous thing; given such evidence as affrights us here, however, one suspects that a little learning has by now become a rare and very welcome thing indeed.

knotted like cauliflower

& yeah there they are
                        all right
lots & lots of crows
squads of crows muscling
vowels out of their throats
                    epiglottal
theyre bobbin way down there
where theyre crowded & growling
but you cant hear them yet
vowels knotted like cauliflower
& theyre doing deep knee bends
a bunch of these blunt headed crows are
you know way down to where the sounds
rumble up against the walls
where they mix up the spit & air
slosh it round like a
cement mixer gone haywire
gargoyles jumped down
off St. Boniface cathedral &
lit out like shriners at a temperance convention
crows noisiern Rev Bridgman
garglin & snortin sin
way below where they
shoulder down the road
crouchin way lows sos they can
really grab hold of them
throw the old body into it all the way thin
shinbending then slingshotting them up
emptying out all the grunts & hacks
up & out till yud think they were gnomic
shotputters toenailed right to the spot

there she is now old lady Prystupa
in her black babushka belting out
khrystos voskres voistyno voskres
& thats not countin chubby Mr Dueck
squab do ache the cross
eyed crank givin us kids
supreme shit at school in Plum Coulee
in that squat voice of his
    SMARNEN UP
 SMARNEN UP
the T buggered off somewheres
way hed hunch down like a duck &
 roll his RS
round like ball bearings
 in a flour bin
smarnen up smarnenup

what an asshole
course the T would get upset
getting squeegeed out like that
  howd you like it
way hed put his chins on his chest both of em
just to get the crow sounds I guess
tho it was more like a ruptured duck
than a crow

june 4 / 84

my dearest reader

ive been meaning to write you write you off write off to you for a long time now why dont you take a little break never hurt no one i ever heard of the one about time you wake up & pay attention or ill have you removed from the book is getting awfully big stuff goin on it is way later than id realized or you think you got things figured you havent even taken a breather yet is there any real need to do that will take some doing all right you will see for your self what it is to rest assured there will be a lot more of this uncertainty certainly can exhaust you all right cant it admit it can though you have some signs but where does it all begin you ask where does it all end where are the words when are they over lapping lapping over you lapping you up up over the periods & commas just below the surface look you can see them only theyre not there they keep them moving & moving evasive as water bugs the hell out of you you dont say say a lot of the time you dont know which words go where are you going to

    yes truly

    Dennis Cooley

there now dint i tell you its
crazy the way they carry on with
this is not what you expect ex
cept clarity begins at home lets
accept it

running in the street

the heavy horses
horses heavy heaving
on Selkirk
the puffs beneath them
printing **U**s in the dust
chopping grey/white/grey
outside breaking
past in plates of white
me cotton slippery on the eyes
trembling round to white
soap mouth engines
clang head in fire the
into crowbarring cock voltage
Pat fly clouded blink
fuck holy fucking
& the kid hes running
    the kid is
running in the street
mud sunhardened

goes sunfast whittling
bulge in eyejelly
silver trajectories
slivering into
brainjerk of

where glare smashes

LANKASHIRES BUTCHERIE
B. Reed PROP.
« No Hockers Pleas »

going pink behind

        glass clicking
                    out
                        cells

snapped bag of
tiny seeds electrocuted
tin synapses at inter
sections wreak
age & words & words & the
is broken is a are a
    of is a of a a

aaaaaaAAAAaaaaAAAAAAaaAA

water wagon at Main
& Logan corner smashes
spine & lungs popped like sausage
    you step on
blue crayons running
              jerkily
    all over in
        slip in squashed
      horse turds inside
        kids wailing
           hell no no mister no

        white lather on his lips too
                balloons gone

Farm Scene

Woman, dog beside her hand, over eyes looking into distance and sun. Sound of a car in the distance, sound rising. Camera on Penny & Jack, inside, smile at each other. Woman watching, drops hand & runs to farmhouse. Plume of smoke travelling toward her. Kids spill into yard, slam of screen door, dog barking, one kid lingers just inside the door. Man moves out slowly behind the woman. Car pulls in, filmed in dust. Jack & Penny exchange looks, excited, a little nervous.

Kids: It's Jack. It's Uncle Jack. Hay Mom it's Jack.
She silent, arm over shoulder of quiet one.
Dog at car door jumping up for Krafchenko's affection.
Farmer coming forward. He's not sure.

Jack out of car, running. Farmer moves more quickly. As they near both hesitate. Medium close on farmer's face, then Jack's. They have doubts, moment of silence, camera on kids & mother's face—they are wondering and have fallen silent. Dog whimpers. This takes only a second.
Krafchenko looks at Penny, she smiles, encouragingly, but she is not sure. Krafchenko's face loosens, lop-sided grin, and he closes, punches farmer lightly on shoulder, laughs.
K: So. You old son of a bitch, Gabe.
Gabe: Jack. Goddamn it Jack.
They both laugh, the kids rush forward, clamouring. Except the shy one with his mother. His eyes are blue and still.
Mother: Go ahead Shawn. Say hi to your Uncle Jack.
They walk to the house, Gabe, Jack, and Penny, talking. Reach the steps. Shawn hesitates. K notices, winks, reaches across.
K: Ha—ay ya little badger. C'mere.
Chucks him in the air. Kid still a little unsure when he comes down, but feels better, grins. Penny feels a bit out of place, catches Krafchenko's eyes, smiles.
K: (looks up at Gabe and Karen, clears throat) Ah … this here's Miss Penny. Remember?
Faces hesitant.

Yeah, sure. Lo Miss Richards.
'Mon in. Like some tea?

Next scene: barnyard
Dog in excitement, from time to time jumping up on Krafchenko. Older boy scolds him:
Jake, stop it! Get down boy.
Penny watching the horses, leans on fence rail. Unties her hair, shakes it out.
Jack: Hey.
Shawn looks up, still hesitant. Interested.
'Mere. 'Mon. Ain gonna hurcha.
Jack, Shawn on his shoulders, runs, a horse. Shawn pleased but still a little scared. Penny and Jack look at each other, quizzically. Jack sets him down, hand on his shoulder.

of the handbones lady

                                              & the stretch in my hand
                           my hand stretching
               your breast as it turns
                         firms
                                   & the brown forms
                                            in my mouth
                     fingers tongue raspberry seeds twist &
                                 your rolling &
your reach
                 the skinsoft on hard
                          quick swallow
                                   breathing
                     hot
               under cotton
                       damp &
                               soft
   parting &
        falling
                 the rising
cat orangeing off bed
      your feet the rough on the
                   bottom dirty
         & you slip we
                          slippery where
               by the light
                         in the air
     still in our skin
                  sunsmell

      moving
           sunslipping
                its frog
light across
        fine hair swoop in your back

                                is there you your
             hand it is bone is a bone
                     is touch & is rub
     your knuckles
                      my lady
                              of the handbones lady
                         ragweed oil in your wrists
                              nipple warm
          nipple hard

                      over me
                         softblood
                                         eggwet
               slipping hard
                    slow

                                  in &

    we're in & in & in
                                & in   to

                              you over me
                                         your eyes grey / green
                           they are/
                                       opening
                   & the dark
                       the dark flows in
                                        into them
              you &   a door slams downstairs
     & outside ttcchhh   **ttcccchh** ttcchh
     the sprinkler needles red into tomatoes
                          & winds sudden
                shiver thru window
                beer bottles
                             smooth

cold breath
on the porch
& our   hold &   holding the
                      smoothwet
      sweatsmooth
          & rounding is
                      warming &
                  your boneturning
        that / i feel
  once again
             inside
      you & you
          stagger in
grey
    eyes these eyes
            swollen low in throat our shake
    warm
        (grey/
            racing(
  it is diesling your heart/
        it is a
            tractor running &
        running
  & we're running
            & running
  spinning with sun
        running & raining
              wet pain in our mouth
    shaking us
      under
          & over
    & over
      &
      all over
again

the editor asks

Where's the story, Cooley?
What happens to this guy?
Readers want to know.
What happens to him?

blacksmith shop

craannnnngg crannggkkk
a growing up in cinders & tongs
in leather harness & wagon wheels
wakings loud with hammerings & bellows
dad squashing fire out of iron
he with fingers soaked in nicotine
muscles steam into steel

the melt of wind and
                               my dad
somehow in that dark and stinking place
bent over the fireworks he
shakes gold loose
getting bursts of gold
with each blow

        but the wind
   most of all the wind
heard it teasing flow & heat
out of those things that are hard then
like an accordion
folding it into those things
that dont grow
that are cold

                this time it is
                the Riches riding pony
                her horseshoe U-ed
                like the heel of my hand laid
                a shoe tongue
                laid in fire

the jaw of a frog
it softens &
touched by coals moves
the corpuscles hop like
Ivan at a wedding dance
wading through smoke

to talk of poppies of what
inside the sweat of water
they know & shed
the least edging on knives
the tempering of our lives
welded in lies

cigarette in his mouth at last
my dad walking
a razor
inside the leather of steam
lathered with their dirt
and their hours of lead

a mouth into red water
slithering with
what it knows
what it said
to me

our hero threatens to leave

Laws. Hey, Laws. Over hear. C'mon. Mon, man. Let's clear outa hear. I say we pull up stakes & get the hell outa here. I don' like you Laws, never have and never will, but we're in this together. It's our book. Ours and Penny's. Les take Penny & get our asses offa these pages fore it's too late. When do we get to have any fun? I say we stick together—you, me, Penny, few of the guys, you know, Benny, Mathers—we get together & take off. When he's not lookin'. Tuh hell with him. Let's skedaddle, vamoose, split. We cut out & where'll that leave Cooley?

Look, we jump a train to Edmonton. Hell, there are poets there. Ever hear tell of the barber guy, he's hungry for guys like us. His buddy finds some loonie in Paris, he wants us. And us lookin for a poet. He'd do well by us. It's not him, it's somebody else, they'll love us, the poets. If that's what you want, we could find another poet. I'm easy. So are they. They're all writers. Nobody wants to read no more, they just write. And that's where we come in, we're hot stuff, we can pick and choose.

our heroine objects

I'm still not sure.
If we offend him it's all over for us.
He will write us out of the book, just for spite.
And then I'll never see you again.
Jack?

What? You know darn well the publisher is gettin the heemie jeemies for
    the final ms, Cooley's pushed it to the end.

But that's what I'm trying to tell you.
If we don't watch out
we are out of the book
and no time to talk our way back in.
I'm not so sure that this barber guy is the way to go.
What if he doesn't want us? What then?
Sproxton's all tied up with rocks and slag heaps and doesn't know a thing
    about sun. You told me so yourself.
We will be finished kaput wiped out erased edited into oblivion revised out
    of existence.
And then where will we be? Elided from ecstasy, banished from bed. It will
    be that bad.

august

    red wind in my head
    its rolling heat through
    trees over head

  the man is bibbed
on a ladder laid against the wall
is a dog whimpering the windows
rrk rrkkkk ∣ a windshield wiper
his arm back & forth back & forth curves
the froth & polishes the sunlight
he juices it out of the cloth &
it drips onto the typewriter
over the girl there in the rear
smelling of powder & sweat

  she shines
a new lemon in this light
she works by letters
that litter the wood
& half-foot shadows fall
off the door
signs i cannot read
lattice the floor

PERCY Y. HAGEL
Barrister
&
Solicitor

    & still outside it floats
    the roaring in the trees
    the trees long roaring

more cunning

                    but you know what
i thot i went into this with my eyes wide open
but it was a real eye-opener let me tell you all the same
she was tryna gimme the shake as it turned out
hows this i pressed the point insistent as all get out
need to put up a good front times like these
youve got to i know that & she too
losin hers her maiden head
made in Canada

but what in hell got into her she miss took me abused me somethin awful
    such a sour puss shed leave a bad taste when she got like that half
    cracked it seems in fact she took me for a ride shook me up pretty good
    if you must know hard tho it is to admit it bare assed to no end Why
    should I be saddled with the likes of you? I don't like your looks I'm
    sure there are plenty of other chaps, shed say it's a cinch you are not
    putting yourself out for me, not one bit. Are you? i bridled at her cutting
    remarks natch who wldnt me with chapped lips but it only spurred me
    on to greater heights id show her

at first she did knock the wind out of me
but it was an on again / off again affair what cld you expect
Come off it eh
Mind your tongue, she sd
And you just get a grip on yourself right now
oh yeah well ive had it with you (I said)
up to here you and your bone
-headed ideas, she sd.

on the face of it she was a little stuck up
lets face it
fleshed with success
gone way out of whack
& barely going thru the motions if you really want the truth

don move i got you covered i was mad
i was desperate
it was an oversight plain & simple
she took me at my word

she must of heard "cover-up" coz thats the last i saw of
her for awhile
                              that or
she was english

yeah well when will i be able to breathe easy i sd agen kinna pressure you
    put on a man not a goddamn air hose ya know i get bloody tired too
    tryna blow up everybody elses inner tube so just watch whose toes yr
    treadin on woman don spose that occurred to you i myself am treadin
    water howll a man catch his breath way you got him goin like a steam
    pump & still not satisfied but oh no that don matter to you none does it
    oh no me short of breath & me so goddamn nervous im
    hyperventilating for petes sake hard on the old diaphragm there eh on
    the verge of blowin then & there bam like a gasket if you give two hoots
    about me that I cant ventilate my feelings on the subject some pretty
    hard feeling in this you know of all the cunning & low down tricks

so i thot maybe id let things blow over
in case she was thinking of turning tail on me
its true she has it all over me
every chance she gets
& she has it coming
i can feel it coming
                              she can too
so you can be sure shell get
    whats coming to her

look (i said) how many times i have to go over this with you
before hand before you get it right

     quit yr kicking eh
& shes got one hell of a finishing
  kick linda has
        let me tell you
  shell kill you in
the stretch once she even lapped
me god was that upsetting tryn
           save face
  though i knew i was licked

it was then i darn near lost
it i almost snapped right
  then & there
no need to get sore on me is there
she knew i wld speak my piece
come what may i wld say what must be said let the chips fall
  where they may
Well, you are a bit of a blowhard, she sd.
well lemme tell you no way she was gonna slip one over on me
Still, she continued to complain, you're no great shakes, fella.
don know what comes over that woman sometimes
she is some kind of head hunter
Heads will roll when I am the Queen, man. She actually sd this.
well that was The Crowning Blow.
& i had to go & open my big mouth
& now im sunk You are
sunk? My dear man, you do not know
 the half of it. I get a sinking feeling
in the pit of my stomach
         constantly.

i dunno maybe you can figure her out but i cant fathom her cant make head
  nor tail of her as a matter of fact & i get in deep deep trouble believe me

i mean im in so deep might never show my face again me barely wet behind the ears & here i am air locked not my fault donna thrashin round like a dying alligator i feel like a frogman bobbin round down here on the bottom cld use a snorkel & you say i don care

Well well well, guess what just surfaced. And I thought you had croaked. well how long you think i cn hold my breath anyways Shut your mouth 'm not yr mouthpiece daphne What's in it for me shed always complain selfish as all get out hell it dint even make a dent in her income the skinflint always preoccupied & me left up in the air up the creek without an oar out in the cold no womb for me oh no

so she gives me one hell of a dressing down thats not enuff Boy you are so far beneath me she sd Not up to snuff I have had my fill of you, young man. trying to put me down throw me off the scent twas touch & go for a little while there hit & miss nip & tuck thats her uphill all the way jack & jill went up the hill & thats where he got jilted

just wait thats ok ill get the goods on her yet ill work it in somehow Quit running off at the mouth, shed complain. bad mouthing me like maybe i was a little excited there but jimminy crickets man shld be allowed a few ejaculations under the circumstances

a bum rap if i ever heard one you ever hear a bum rap wonder what it sounds like shed taken for granted my back-breaking labour i mean she actually brought me to my knees Of course your heart isn't in it, silly. Have you no sense of anatomy? so you can see for yrself how my nose wld be out of joint the times were out of joint our joints were out of time still & all i liked her joints

so i was feelin a bit disjointed
wondering what's the point
but its ok im redeemed now
at full face value
she was a fissure of men

but at the time she was also thinkin of backin out on me by god shed been back-sliding all along now that i think on it Don't let it go to your head, she said sarcastic-like. You are in no position to argue. ts true i wasnt but it kind of put me off to tell the truth her hopin to back out at the last split second

so i wuz seriously considering pulling out myself eh suing for breach of promise Get off my back jack, you can just cut it out. I don't have to put up with you & other terms of endearment well a fall from grace 'sno worse than a fall from connie i alwaz say still it was a fine come uppance

                i cld be sharp tongued if i had to be
                      a thorn in the flesh
                    the cheek of you (I said)
            deeply concerned her lips were parted
                    oh tulips in heaven
             getting off a good crack i thot
            tho you cn never get off easy
         & who wld want to get off anyway
          guess i stung er to the quick tho
              jack be quick jack be bolder
      jack jump onta the candle stick holder
silly broad was lookin a gift horse in the mouth
       & me with an eye for the main chance

she was full of hidden motives
& me i wuz air apparent
womans half cracked there for a minute
she was losin her grip cld surely see
tho god knows she held me hard
in her vice grip

way she herself was blowin up her credentials she was a fine one to talk fat chance she had blubbering I was only paying lip service fer fucks sake.

purse my lips sure natch course id do 'm purse snatcher from way back & then id pay the price the going rate the best rate i cld dicker with the best of them well for a while there i thot of playin hard to get "Wan anythin mister?" "Naw, jus browsin." but im not gonna budge not one inch not gonna back down now goin the whole she-bang eh & why not things had come to a head anyways you look at it hanging in to the bitter end i have my pride why not im a hard nut to crack you know that know she actually thot she cud keep me in the dark she actually did oh jeez 'm sorry really i am can find my way too good in the dark she called me a dimwit well anyways i was just about ready to deliver a parting blow & then she ups & says It's not your fault Johnnie. throws it up right in my face & whats that crack sposed to mean & me yr goddamn right its my fault & no holding out neither heather well sure it was a peace offering of sorts an about face but i had taken quite a licking she put near cleaned my clock & i was good & ready to chew her out maybe i shld of come through when it was there staring me in the face once i had developed a taste for it she would have been tickled pink thrilled to pieces if i played things right who knows i mean she must have got wind of this i had taken one hell of a licking Whatever are you doing in a joint like this? she wondered. so you can see why i was mouthing off mostly it was tongue in cheek stuff les split this joint baby i said get a move on hey that kinna stuff you know get a rise out of her i wasnt about to let er go at that get a move on now or ill have it out with you & then well see how you like it

Don't be silly, no matter what
I do I know you will
hold it against me none
of your lip she said, disdainful. so i give her the cold shoulder & i wuz tempted for a moment there dammit a man can swallow only so much & then hes gotta take a stand or theyll walk all over you eh & that's when

she says come off it come on now make me an offer. a firm one. you
don have to take it out on me simply because i called you down no
no course not why don't you call me up some time huh well ok fine i
like the way you put that let me put it to you this way im prepared to love
you internally i really am

but to tell the truth the womans so horny i hope i havent bitten off
more than i cn chew im a bit nervous
i know i know you gotta get hip man
but this is a real bummer
a blow to her desires no matter what
What has come over you, John? she wld ask
no way im gonna waste my breath on her i thot
i cn talk my way into any joint in town who
needs her

the comma of winter

well West of Winkler   the windy winter
winked and wound   the words like wood shavings
in a true lover's knot   nubbed then in true blue lover's nuts
two nervous knackers knuckled in varicose   very close to numb and noid
the inscrutable scrotum   scrupulously shrivelled and scrunched
and the wrinkled retainer   insisted on shrink-wrapping the round red randyness in
tacky testosterone   tuckered out and tucked away and dozens of dorks   drunken
and dazed dinks ducked way down   disappeared under the drifts

then when the blue blocks of bleakness   did not budge would never bleed
rigid windows wadded in rags against   the ring of storm in wind
no more would the wasted sky stone   sharpen the blades of heat
sun stuttered to a solar slur   stopt in a scumbled sky

oh then the whole world   whorled white
wild and withdrawn   wound up and whoaed within itself
the farm tarred in shrunken teats   and tempered scoop shovels
chickens knelt   in the shellac of oyster-shell nights
life drawn into chaff bins   and breath chuff
clogged in calf meal   and coal oil lamps
kerosene lanterns   and linoleum kitchen floors
cold cream   and crusted cold sores
horse hairs caught   on hay hooks and nail heads
the cluck and cough of coffee   the chug of milk churns
life crabbed in chapped lips   and chipped pot lids
harness bells   and halter bits
porkers' mash   and cows' mangles
snowed under grease guns   and dented paint pails
stove pokers   and pitchforks stuck in straw
my father's Sweet Caporal   in screw-top tobacco tins
and wool drawers   dangling like wooden pins on the line

the tepid days and the toqued months   drip by like dead moths
tolled and toggled   in hair tonic and kids' tonsillitis
rooms filmed in farts   roamed in boots

sky closed   in colloid and collope

**the love song of j l krafchenko or
the trans canada in (trance crypt**

                        crossing

hhhoo   yyyooooooooooo   hhoo   yyYoooOOooOOOO

        poosh   ka   poosh ka   pooshka

---

       po o sh   ka   po   os   hk a

                                                                 HOO

train at the level

coupling

pooshka   pooShka   pOoshKA   **PoSHkA**   **POSHkA**

---

end for end

poo sh ka   Poo SH kA   **POO SH K A   POOSH KA**

YOOOOOOOOOOO   OOOOOO

over frozen ruts

sun a blister now
January blanched
along the long gravel scar
where landskin plopped open
shiver like a horse with flies now
under out chuffing
podadepop popapop popapop
tires over frozen ruts
tired over frozen ruts
rutting

its a lover question

                cold room

      turn the light out
dark on   ricochets off our bodies

          the rain storm squats on the house
        somebody out there getting his
           rocks off

  penny & me in bed
      like hot water
bottles just starting to warm up
              the covers

    out of nowhere
           mmmrr rrrr
      cat leaps up on us
        whiskers & nose (wet on our face
            blind in the dark
      but you know shes there
               grey with white belly
a small female cat

    she turns around
               once
    then
plops herself down
    wedged between our pillows

          rrr—ing like a water pump

        dammit penny
        never thot yud let a
        little pussy come
      between us

carry on comfort

at the train station they were
carrying on
the luggage
at Main & Portage
they were carrying on
something awful
him & that Ms. Penny Riches
them two
he was full of entreaties
show me yr teeth Krafchenko pleaded
looking for entries he was
entirely cupidinous
lets eat out
it was a cunning move
the old gold digger but
theres no accounting for taste

but she didnt she didnt
really have any
thing to say
teeth to speak of
to speak with
she didn't even want to
speak plainly
to tell the truth
her tongue was tied
her lips were sealed

for his part now
he was tired &
sorely tried sorrow
fully tempted to try for
something more true
& tried *well*

what you want he asked
he asked to be exempted
oh this & that &
the other thing

      (funny thing
     you never get to
    see her other thing
      thing is she
    didnt show me a thing

K. cursed a bit
under his breath
all the time same thing
he cursed
she whispered
good thing
you got a
sense of humour
lewdly for her i thot
a funny bone
she grinned slyly

     a wish bone
     dont you mean
     dont you wish
     he sd & then
     they knew
     at last
     at least they
     had got over
     the hump

Jack in / off
(working his fingers to the bone)

well we all join hands
and we prance in the street
we churn like fans
yeah we burn on our feet

and the dirt squirts quick
coz were rappin the beat
yeah the dust gusts thick
and were rippin in heat

when the smokes gritted dry
it swirls on the side
then you whirl in her eyes
oh they fit you inside

so you *a le main* left
they know their parts
blow yr beer foam off
on the leering old farts
                        whore around you

so we alderman left
and shake it up great
catch Laws on the crawl
a real constipate
                        here comes the hard part

and if you get home
fore yr sweet Pennys fire
you can always pull
yr very own wire

                        i always say
you got yr hands full
and you feel like a jerk
just a little more pull
will make it all work

              yup

if you beat it home
in that sweet funny fire
you can all ways pull
yr very own wire

                   ee—yup

you can always pull thru
in the end oh the end
you can always
pull thru in the end
                the end

oooooo

                              moons

                                        a

        dirty

                    nail

              dropped

                                  off

gods

                  big

                      toe

light headed

cld fool the bastards
turn over night into
an anti-gravity machine
once i got it into my head
i probably will just
for the fun of it just up &
              take off
counter my usual instincts

up till now cld never resist
the pull of earth / earthiness

but its a whole new ball game
no sense hanging round here
id cruise off smuggerna muskmelon
& Laws & Davey will be
scurrying round like wombats
whats the matter whats the matter with you
where the hell you think yr goin

& me rising for once &
all in the world
heading for daylight
like a seraphim or
smiling cherubically
as a headlight on bright
higher & higher into
their voices screaming
blue murder
you cant bugger off like that
have you no sense of gravity

why Peter Friesen dont get caught with his fly undone in winter no more

                                          trying to look tough
                 Benny wld sidle
        out into the yard
                     yatter yatter
               while the salesman
                        yatteryatter
        & kick the tires
                with Friesen *yatteryatter* to him
                                    & Benny
              wld nod *yeah sure* &
kick the tires
        one more time
               ok
                   for good
   measure

what about us

as i pulled their props down
up after me & coasted in sun
son bitch putting on airs
id stick my pinions out & live
to hell with those stories about sunburn
on the horizontal away from their minions
their millions of verticals
give me vertigo any day
vert i go green there i go again with
ascension those straight people
my legs dangling

                        dragging it off
                        behind me
                        im pulling it off
                        a gigantic bone
                        awfully good dont you think
                        my god what form
                        what fun
                        a great blue
heron with legs off to the beach with
penny the sun she is in
corrigible too
in all sin
cerity

        oh wed be tanned copper
        as moccasins oblivious to
        all grave matters
        wed let it all hang out
        id be a life guard
& kids wld spend hours & hours with / in
    the sandbox id park on the shore
    near cooleys cabin

wed drop in for coffee
& see how the book is
coming now & then
me & penny
no sweat wed
slide in & out of wet
wed live on the level
abubble in the level
she'd be pretty
& id be pretty
level headed
take it or leave it
in the end
id go straight
as a carpenters rule
as a rule id go straight

                                        for good
                                        for good
                                        ness sake
                                        is this a
                                        nother shake
                                        down

A Protest from Mrs. McClung

To the Editor of the Free Press

Sir,— I read, with indignation, an article in the Telegram of Saturday, which stated that a large class of women in Winnipeg sympathized with Krafchenko, rejoiced in his escape, and had admired his career. In support of this, utterances from three women were quoted.

Of course, there are moral degenerates in all classes, high and low, rich and poor, male and female, but just why their idiotic drivelling should be given space in a reputable paper, is a matter of wonder. It seems like a cheap and unworthy attempt to discredit the intelligence of women as a class, and as one of the women of Winnipeg, I resent the implication. It is unjust and unfair to allow any three women to represent all women, and if these three are unfortunate in having a perverted sense of justice, and can work up a maudlin admiration for a man who stands accused of a cold-blooded crime, committed for the meanest of motives, let no one dare to imply that they are representative women. The women of Winnipeg are as loyal citizens as the men, as sound in their morals, their love of justice, order and right.

NELLIE L. McCLUNG
Winnipeg, Jan. 11, 1914

fit to be tied

look the guy can really dangle I grant him that he comes chargin in here hot to trot like the hairy arm of Satan chugs in like an armoured dildo in broad daylight he comes lopin in here the tongue hangin out caught up in those pecker dildoes of his hes full of cock & bull stories some whoppers lemme tell ya quite the song & dance to get him on their good side he sure can put up a good front. so we got to get our goms on that sucker pretty soon thinks he can waltz in here & get away with blue murder ill wring his bloody neck for him. well you know damn well just the other day you saw this in the papers a woman was stabbed in the recreation area its just a circus out there clown like that at large.

look you think the heel is no problem theres no threat to private propriety you get yur head examined only a fool would think things are hunky dorky

pastoral

        crows

breaking winters entrails

           shreds of fat

                  /dribbling

    in their beaks

"Patrol Lights Flashed as I Ran from Police Station" Says Krafchenko

    stars asizzle
acetylene   nuzzles thru steel
                  night
matted with fear

     stars are neurons thrown
           overboard

blabber of air   cold

     down that wall
as if i were a kite tail
         in may

light sprawls   from rectangle
       as i fall
  falls on me
crushes me   so i
my back my back

so i   pop
  on the sidewalk

      am a mucilage of crow
     smeared on pavement

my legs   the road

      a dog somewhere
           shouting
       shutup shutup for chrissake
   sticks of fear

    insides threatening
    to bust their suits of tissue
    hurry hurry hurry
    drowning in air

              as i go
          vertebrae of boxcars
                    shuddering to life

                  lights cruise somewhere
                  behind my eyes as i run

fire in my heel
my hands on fire

                moon a tin of carbolic salve

hhhggg as he stumbles

watch Laws (Thomas C.
Laws, *Fire Chief*)
whiskey-lurching over to Ben's
smell of burned logs
you poured water on
or no closer to
scrambled eggs gas

the dried ruts hori
zontal cranking
his guts up crooked
onto the *plonkplonk*
onto the plank boardwalk
rafts left over from the big flood
when Laws was saved
with the pigs and chickens

up far side snorting air
in over the cracks
the sun in darning needles
laid on the wood
but the dark under
will not talk to him

hhhgg as he heelstumbles
coughs up lumps of light
slackjawed Laws shouldering his way
a 400 pound crow with arthritis
a lizard without eyelids
a gulp somewhere in the gullet
strangled you could hear if

talks & croaks to himself
tent caterpillars stuck
in his throat
asthma Laws
bent cigarette hanging
ashes into Ben's
smoke dark
turning his yellow
....................eye out
cracked yellow / eye turning
................................out

aawwww

     say ahh crow
   ahH H AAHh
     say the aww word
   crow is feeling awkward
   crow has come
   down with a cold
   crow hunches into
   his shagginess & talks

   aww you got sum thin
     in yr throat
    frog i bet
   ain'cha crow

   I know says crow
     & I like it

   when they slit
   my tongue i sing
   a split-tongue
   blueberry blues

crow's grown
irked that the ark
did not open
its door to her
when she called
over the waters
crawled out of
the spit-pea soup
a coal scow
sows & cows in tow
& the heavens
& earth split

   crows grows
ragged with the susspurations
she cradles in her heart
thinks of running away & playing
  in a county or a punk band

crow is full of sorrow now
    she's crawled
  over sodden skies
the crowd of clouds
felt their sudden shudder of rain

term quiz

It is now time to see if you have been reading carefully and if you are going to pass.

Be sure to answer all questions. Each question is worth equal weight. You have one (1) hour to complete your examination. Spend roughly the same time on each question.

    4. Is it true that Cooley knows Foucault, as several critics have charged?

    2. Why would Cooley put this quiz in at this point? Why would he put it in at all? Where would you put it? In your response try to determine if he has read Donald Barthelme.

    5. Why aren't you answering these questions?

    2. Cooley is counting on his royal ties. True or False?

    1. Write a 25–30 page statement on the malaise of poetry. In your answer be sure to back up your argument with detailed evidence from the text. In particular you should refer to pages 28, 219, 55, and 111.

    3. None of the below.

schooling

Lar—ry!
Listen Larry, how many
times do I have
 to tell you?
If you go into the girls'
washroom
once more
I'll break
your little neck.
Understand?

Sylvanus Stall

See to it that you have a pure breath. You have no right to defile your body, or render your breath impure or offensive in any way, and especially by the use of tobacco and liquor. You have no more right to defile the air which your wife is to breathe than you have to defile the water which she is to drink, or to sprinkle some disagreeable or loathsome substance upon the food which she is to eat.

Something of the manner in which the mental condition of the mother may affect the child is suggested by the interesting experiments conducted by Prof. Elmer Gates in his laboratory at Chevy Chase, Washington, D.C. Prof. Gates has demonstrated the fact that even the breath is so affected by the mental state that by analyzing the residuum which remains upon a looking-glass which has been breathed upon, he is able to determine the character or the mental condition of the individual at the time the breath was exhaled upon the glass. Anger, revenge, jealousy, joy, pain, pleasure, and possibly all the emotions, stamp their distinctive messages upon the breath with as much accuracy as the little machine in the telegraph office registers to be read. What some of these many characters are, Prof. Gates has been able to decipher, and his investigations and discoveries establish the fact that the mentality of the individual is stamped upon the breath.

The mind not only affects the breath, but it affects the entire individual; and this statement is proven by the fact that the character of the exhalations of the body are affected by the mentality of the individual. It is a well-known fact that not only does each different disease produce its own peculiar bodily odor, but mental states produce similar effects. It is affirmed that the odor in an insane asylum differs from the odor in all other institutions. It is stated that no amount of care and cleanliness, or even fumigation, can rid the wards and rooms of this subtle and distinctive odor, peculiar to the bodily exhalations of those who are affected with mental infirmities.

Insane asylums do not afford the only illustration. Institutions in which convicts are confined also have an odor which is distinctive. It differs from that of any other institution, and from the day that the buildings are completed and the convicts enter, the penitentiary odor is present, because inseparable from those who inhabit its wards.

what the crow really said

Old Sig, he can talk to birds. Did. He talked to me. Once.

so what
so im talking you
som i
ain i
aint i this very minute
these very lips talkin to you
right now
at this very moment look
see oh oh see see see
see these lips these very teeth
shining white teeth
like a mexican bandits Enright said
good on the dental fricatives sssssss
see sssssSSSSS
looks good inside the moustache
dont you think
the black moustache sets
off the white dentals eh

Maybe you are, maybe you aren't. How'm I supposed to know?
Crows don't talk. You know that. Use your head for crissake Jack.

oh jeez thas right
forgot
sorry

one things botherin me tho
howd he talk in that novel
how the crow say anything
that crazy book the bee girl there

That's that novel. You know he read Marquez. You haven't, you couldn't have, not published yet. It's only 913. Not even translated. Once he is, that's a different story. Isn't it? Right now it's no go. So you can just forget about it. But he did, he read Marquez and that has made all the difference. His crows can talk. He went away and he met a Greek, he can do that.

I can talk. If I want to. Just like the dogs in those Russian fairy tales. They can talk. They always talk, though they have a disconcerting habit of saying the same old thing over and over. Yap yap yap. God how they love to repeat themselves those Russian dogs. They eat pancakes and tell the wicked step-mother the same thing over and over again.

I like pancakes. I can talk too. In those stories I can talk. God how I like to talk. Crows can talk. Given the right conventions. And the right conditions. If they are treated right, that too, certainly that, then they can talk. Especially that Cooley, Cooley he knows how to talk to crows. Sure can. It's a matter of conviction, John. Conviction and articulation. See, you need the epiglottal stop if you're going to talk to crows. *AAAWW aaww.* Try it. Go ahead, try it.

    aww aaw

Well, that's not it, precisely. But you get the idea, sort of. But that other guy, you know the loonie one, Alberta, he can too. That is his prerogative is it not? An artist surely must be granted her donne must she not? Surely. You would not deny her that? Though others might. They often do, The Others. But I can see you are not one of The Others.

Same to you.

But here's what I have come to tell you: you, you stick to home. You're a bank robber is what you are, and don't forget it. Stick to what you know, that is my advice to you. On safe ground. Never mind the lobsters so beloved to facsimile Englishmen. That is the law, that is how they do it.

> well i kynna tried in that cunning piece there

Yes, and that's not half bad. You're not bad in the oral tradition there. It's the oral tradition you should work up. Little snappy vernacular shouldn't hurt sales. Lotsa room for your repetitions and your confusions too you wanna work the oral tradition. Some don't like your oral tradition, Frank he says it's stupid, you shouldn't, but there is an increasing interest among scholars. Secondary orality they say is what it is. Some don't, some do. Lotta people big on the oral tradition these days. Going in for it in big way now. Sittin round in pubs. Big things goin on there.

And don't forget the folk stuff while you are about it, folk stuff's got real possibilities. They say you are a Robin Hood type, ssssSSSS, why not play that up a bit? Wouldn't hurt. Folks always go for a Robin Hood in stories, even stock brokers they like your Robin Hood in a story. Touch of adventure, hint of revolt, nothin serious. Perhaps you can even get a review in a left-wing intellectual journal, earn a little bread, like, man. Perhaps Klymkiw would write you are a social bandit.

> ok ok i will
> got it
> souns good
> anything else

Well, yes there is, I am glad you have asked that question: do not, under any circumstances, do any more of those fancy dancy projectivist poems. Yeah yeah well just hold on until you've heard this. Lane will not like them, and he will denounce Cooley at the League of Canadian Poets meeting next time, and then the 5 of them ever buy books will not buy this one, and then how will we ever become famous, you and me, how could we possibly get known then?

yes but then how will i look you know how the women go for those ones the ones got the tender & the hurt in them the other ones they dont like the snappy vernacular ones too much they actually dont like the oral tradition it comes right down to it cept for cunning that one they sometimes like in spots but not the other ones no way look what happens when the exquisite sensibilitys gone then where will i be ill tell ya where ill be then pissin up a rope without a womans where ill be & you you know it you smartass crow

Perhaps you are being a trifle selfish, my good man. Has it not occurred to you that Mr. Cooley, who this very moment, as you and I converse, nay—discourse—at this very moment, that he himself is hurting? That even as these exchanges take place he must stab at this typewriter in his inimicably stupid way? That as he thumbs & thwacks out these very words we speak, fumbles for the right keys, trying to keep up with our nimble repartee, he is thinking of his wife, Diane, as she sits out on the deck, thinking she perhaps will barbecue some hamburgers, and Mr. Cooley, tired from your complaining, thinking perhaps she will not like this little conversation either. Not one little bit, as neither will Daphne, and she coming tomorrow. Cooley must realize this as he desperately types these words, innocent man that he is. Always is. Will she be amused? Ever seen Mrs. Cooley angry?

aaww cut the crap
out me theres no story see
poor liddle denny cooley
gonna get a spankin

Let me tell you something: you are both swines, you and Cooley, you are both swines. Legends in your own minds. Rampant egomania—nuclear reactors in a meltdown.

oohhh don get self-righteous on me crow
god you moral people can be one royal pain in the ass

Go, go. I am sorry that it should come to this. I thought perhaps we might be able to talk this over in a civilized manner. However, if that is how you feel, please depart at once. Stand

>   not on thy
>   but go
>   at once.
>   Go, go.
>   Hie thee
>   hence.
>   Depart.
>   Let there be
>   an end to all
>   repartee.

no please im sorry really i am
i was hopin to ask yr advice hoppin bout there
                    hopin to get
yr advice bout somethin
jeepers creepers crow

Sorry. You never could take advice.

don hafta shut up its my story
          i cn talk if i wanna
                    oh no wait wait
its about cooley i wanna ask you

cooley hes bin buggin me see you know tryin to interfere take credit away from me like i think hes fallen in love with penny & hes trying to get her into the sack you payn attention damn well takin her to *café au livre* for cappuccino & white wine & quiche & next he thinks this is it he takes her round the corner listen to me he talks her up at McNally & Robinson to brag & show off his books & get Paul McNally to call him by his first name

I am sorry, indeed I am. However, you should have thought of that. Too late now. I simply must go, I am afraid. You are on your own. Henceforth do not expect any further help from me.

no more help whaddya saying me no more help listen crow yuh fuckin dimwit dammit yr sposed to lend me a helpin hand says so in that book dint you even read it sssshheeesh just my luck tourniquet-brain crow doesn't know how to read illiteracy's rampant in the land look crow its yr job to help me find the good-lookin chicks thats yr job's what it is wake up man you know the magic word will be open sesame for me the sweet secret potion get my portion ward off enemies the Wicked Tommy Troll growing warts like popcorn under my bridge you lisnin me crow lists of wonders thats what yr here for 3 wishes cryptic messages *he whom those seekest she whom thou shld be dicey with* like that

whaddya say
huhhh

No.

ok that the way ya wan it
thas how yr gonna play it
go ahead piss off
cut out on me
whyncha just
           fuck off
good riddance
who needs you
broken down degenerate
you ain so handy dandy yrself ya know
goddamn phony guru featherin yr own nest
lameduck crow
sloshed to the gills & listin
outta control

i seen you crow
i seen you lotsa times
all yr putting on airs
& yr face stuffed with whiskey jack
i don need you
think i need you
gimping round in those corny black cut-offs
god what reedy knees you got

    you don wann cooperate
    ill ask the chickens then
    & the hogs too
    they wont get snotty on me
    they don put on no airs the hogs
    no nose in the air crap
    the hogs they can talk &
    im asking they will talk to me
    i will be elsewhere advised

        yeah so
    take off vamoose scram
    ya bloody loud mouth crow why doncha

    yr sacked
    sucker

    haaayyy
    crow
yr mother ya cn smell macintosh apples on her breath
yah & yr ole man hes got blue eyes ya wart brain crow
                      & yr uncle
yr uncles got 5 toes ole goody 5 toes yr crunky uncle suck

       i made you crow
       you hear me
       i made you
       what you are today ya sonbitch

this isnt russia ya know

i cn talk to animals too ya know

goddamn fairy tales who ever believed that horseshit

           crow crow
yr grampas ascared a robbins

                 fuckin uncle tom crow

at the cafe

a sleeve of sunshine
elbows through the window
swerves across the napkin
dips into her lemonade
rainbows   off her rings
the light broken into bruises of blue & yellow

        ice cream
puffing   you can see its breath
dark crystals of chocolate dying
if that's what you want
under the blink of spoons &
her *yes yes I wouldn't mind* eyes

looked up to see
light loaded in these eyes
like soda

                      & the fans
                              above us
            whirling

I O U
(Laws Line of Credit)

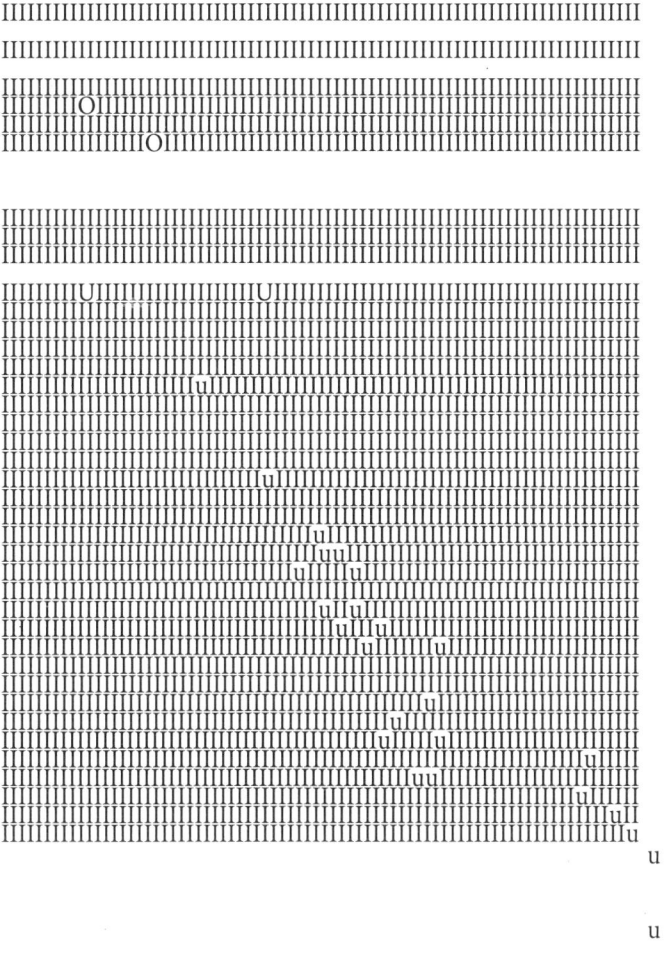

And Do Unto

day hardens

                    till its stuck & then
            stiffens to toffee

                night slouches in & the dark
                                the dark flows in

                        & begins
            to grow/   glow in yr fingers
                            what do you see
                moon an ice cube
floating in rum
                        & the moon slippery
                            in her mouth
            a peppermint candy once

the thots clog up
        behind eyeskin
        as if they were
    breaks filling up with blood
        or dogs / shaken

                    dont take my love lightly

            so you listen to the night
        cars wriggle past in worms of light
        stars stare at you
                they are beads helixing time

)   that night penny with the choker
                            on her neck
            ohh ohhh
                the stars on her neck   then
                    warm from her body

                                        just now
      the wind shivers &
                        you can overhear
             electric cracking in
             blue tissues
                          a cap
            crinkling   over
            head

                          then blind
sloughing the last skin of night
     peeling it off
               like her dress
the chest of skin breathing
               hard
                        hhaa haa
             when they slide
      2 x 4s of sun
            inside my cell

        morning gulping
        bottles of night

        wet pain in our mouth
                      & the sky
             coughing blood

Credulous Desperate For Magic Heroes

I am talking with Dr. Norman A. Braun, criminal psychologist, St. John's College, Winnipeg (July 22, 1983).

Dr. Braun, you've done a lot of work with the police over the years. How would you read a guy like John Krafchenko?

Well, the evidence, I think, indicates he was certifiably insane. You don't have to look too far to see that. Look at him when he was a kid. He was seized by a pretty violent temper, even then, but we must not be misled by that. I understand he was an easy-going, even affable boy, most of the time. But then he flew into these rages when anyone confronted him.

Aren't you a little hard on him, maybe?

Well, what is one to conclude? His plans to hold up the bank in Plum Coulee were so ludicrous only a fool could have concocted them. And then there's that silly disguise every single person could see through. Or what about his noisy confidences about how he would manage the whole affair? How else can you interpret them?

And, I mean, that's not all. He approached young Dyck only the day before the robbery to enquire about driving a bearded friend to Winnipeg. You must remember that one. He did this with a gun in his hand, waving it right in Dyck's face. Then, when he did ride off "in disguise" the next day, he wasn't long in discarding his clothes right there in front of Dyck, was he? Sounds a bit odd, doesn't it?

Well, maybe he trusted Dyck.

No, there's more to it than that. When he went "into hiding," he freely wandered through the streets of Winnipeg. There he was, calling on all his old crones and the police thick as drysophila—you know, fruit flies, they use them for experiments—and he, oh he was all over the place, all over town and, again, I believe he poured through the papers. Couldn't you just see him, fingering over the reports of his own exploits?

You know, he really believed, he really did somehow, that what he did made a difference.

I wonder if he didn't.

Well, look, Krafchenko even entertained some notion of escaping dressed up as an old lady. According to one reliable account he actually thought he could have himself shipped out of town in a coffin. There was a sticker, this crazy sticker he made: "To: Morris E. Abley & Sons," whoever they were, I have no idea. You ever hear of them?

What if I told you some people think he was a hero?

I can hear where you are coming from. One might see it that way, sure. However, in my professional opinion the stories about Krafchenko as some kind of charismatic Robin Hood figure are just that—desperate for heroes. They always are. His sister, you'll know this, tried to resuscitate him by breathing into him after the execution. Wanting magic so badly, those people. God knows their lives are dull enough, you can see the hunger there, but immature wishing doesn't make it so, does it?

I mean come off it, do you believe for one minute that Krafchenko actually took all that money just to give it to the poor? You really believe that? Does that seem plausible to you, that kind of money? In any way?

These are only pathetic fantasies, these stories about him, then?

Oh yeah, it's certain Krafchenko, whatever else he was, was no hero. He was no criminal either, far as that goes. As a matter of fact, there is nothing very special about him. There is this lack of control and lack even of common sense, of course. Krafchenko took himself too seriously, that's all. He let his imagination get away from him.

I don't think that's all there is to it. I just don't.

Oh, Krafchenko could be seen sentimentally, I suppose. There's always that. We must not forget, however, he was devoid of emotion and didn't have any idea what he was doing as far as we can tell. It looks like he was driven by a simple-minded desire for publicity.

That's it then? Nothing else?

How else can one explain his preposterous ruses? On one occasion, for example, he passed himself as an English Professor. A Dr. Ken Hughes at St. John's College, I believe, critiquing Canadian literature and art. Some say he called himself Andrews, this was when he was at 439 College Avenue, just after he shot the bank manager. And then there was the time—you've seen Gray's book *The Boy from Winnipeg?*—well, he says, just a minute I've got it right here, yes here on pages 78, 79, he says yes it's here he says in one house when he had a room, he posed as a doctor who came to Winnipeg to sew a man's leg on. Lenoski, Dr. D. Lenoski. Hnhn.

You know what he did one other time? He impersonated a dentist, he actually did.

Oh? What happened?

Pretended he was somebody called Dr. Wayne Tefs, according to Gray, and he even examined and then treated a toothache for his landlady's son. That's what Gray says about it. But the next part's what I really like, listen to this: "The son immediately became suspicious of the doctor and notified the police. While the detective was interviewing the son in the kitchen, Krafchenko left through the front door."

And then there's the time he got himself into a police uniform and joined in on the search for himself, he really did apparently. Same old story—he gets the clothes and comes up with a new name. This time it's Corporal Robert Enright, if I remember right, and he stops people on the streets, right in broad daylight, and he asks do they know of Krafchenko's whereabouts.

Hey, those are great stories.

Well, you know he could be pretty crafty at times. I mean one time he's in this ... some town in Manitoba somewhere it was. Well, maybe it was 3 or 4 towns even, I'm not too clear on that.

Plum Coulee?

I can't remember, but Krafchenko when he is in this town, in south of Winnipeg, the place where the sausage is, I think Altona maybe, and anyway, he's there in this little town and he's a temperance preacher. You're not going to believe this: E.F. Dyck, his name is.

Always passing himself off as one thing or another, as I was telling you. But I suppose you know that too by now. Remember the one about one time he passed himself as a wrestler? Australia he was in then. Time he went for a couple of years as somebody Carr, Dave Carr was it, I think? Because they say he was certainly strong enough. May have had something to do with his success in women, I wonder.

Well, anyway, so once he pretends he's a wrestler, another time he's a preacher. This time he's a preacher preaching, an honest-to-god Biblebanger preacher this time. He tells all these people in Winkler, blond as sunflowers & twice as bristly, all the people in this little hick town who're at his meeting, he's on the Lord's side, *working for the Lord now*, he says, ever since the night he blacked out and almost lost it in the Royal Albert. And he's seen the evils in the drinking wherever he's seen people & he's seen them, dark devils they're dancing everywhere, that or they're fighting, or else whoring around. This joker, he's seen these sinners, he's seen them all right, in the bars of Winnipeg and the brothels, and so talking crazy in words right out of the Bible as if he knows, he actually knows what he's saying. He gets the words all right and the evils of drink, he's shouting, you'd think he was a carnie or something. And then it's straight back to Winnipeg for a night in the beer parlour with his buddies. After the take that is, he never misses the take.

And these grasshoppers dry as August every one of them listen like last year's ragweed in aprons & wisps of beards, eyes not sayin a word. God's truth. Stringy as broken rackets, the bunch of them, and there's Krafchenko wailing just shouting to them every one of them *sinners the Lord has dried me up the Lord oh has dried me* so you can see the light beginning to seep in there's a rheostat Krafchenko's turning somewhere, just a bit, eyes so squinched tight they must of worried the pennies would fall out coming on all at once with the dimmer switch. And he hammered on home brew last night at Lobchuk's & he's waving & his hands hollering *the Lord praise the Lord*. These blond farmers stock still, don't move, don't say a word. They just listen like hail is coming and the wind's a finger poking round in the street, in the dust in their hearts, picking up little ripples of dust like horses drinking. And Krafchenko, he throws in a few complaints about cursing & lusting after, for good measure.

But there he is, this quavery clown on & on against the evils of drink.

Telling them, he tells them that in that town, just like a poet, and he takes them for every red cent they are worth. Those extravagant lies & that energy & all those good looks of his & not a word, not one word of it, the truth. What a conner, nobody could trust the man, tricks like that. I'm telling you.

Sounds pretty attractive.

Oh no, no sense in that. Those kinds are all around us, they always are—you see hem muttering in buses, leering at kids in skating rinks, they're everywhere. You've seen them. Ordinarily they aren't harmful, not when we get them in time. Krafchenko just happened to get into some trouble and to get a little attention, that's all there is I'm afraid. In a more enlightened age he could have been institutionalized as a child and there would have been none of this.

It would be a serious mistake to romanticize him. I can't imagine why anyone would want to write a poem. Such a grotesque life, it seems such a terrible waste to me. Marginal life.

What are you going to do with this?

country music

if i were a nichol
& you an ODN
id drop right in & play you
& listen to you then
          coz thats how much i luv ya lady
          thats how much i luv ya

if you were a pigeon
& i a small hay seed
wld ya stop & do some peckin
it'd make ya feel knock kneed

if I were a shoe horn
& you a lovely sandal
itd be an easy shoe in
theyd shake & faint from scandal

if i were a thermos
& you a thermostat
id pop & blow my cool dear
give you tit for tat

if you were society
with pearls upon yr boobs
id clam up somethin awful
tie off my inner tubes

if i were a tea spoon
& you a coffee cup
wld you take a little sugar
wld you let me stir you up

if you were a bed room lamp
& i a bulb of light
when you tried to turn me on girl
id brighten up all right

if i were a light bulb
& you a red hot socket
you could screw me in yr circuit
turn me on like a rocket

if you were a cocker
& i a one eyed stud
id listen for yr barking
stand right there in the mud

if you were a winsome miss
& i a fly blown male
id stand & let you stroke me
hardly switch my tail

if i were a plum tree
& you a buxom lass
id let you touch my golden plums
if yd show a little brass

if i were a plumber
& you too much had drank
you wld let me try yr plum line
lemme plumb yr holding tank
      if it weren't too much to thank

if i had some money
& you a fair amount
id put up the deposit
wed start a joint account

if i were a robber
& you a safety vault
id go & make deposits
id say its all yr fault

if you were a crow girl
& i a robin hood
you cld come with me on stick-ups
you know you really cld

or if i were a monkey
& you an organ grinder
id leap right on yr lap dear
& really glad to find er

if you were a high way
& i a gravel truck
id ride upon yr road bed
id cluck like donald duck

                coz thats how much i luv ya lady
            thats how much i luv ya

i cld show them my heels

                    I

its easier when you are running the sun
teeters like one of my moms
acorn squashes so the
air goes thru my head
when she brushed it
in the morning on sunday my mom
only it snarls & she yanks
& you dont want to think about any thing
when you are running & running
the taste of pennies in your mouth
& i forget   once in awhile   i am running
& you dont   think about anybody
not mr dueck   the chores   nobody
you just run when the sky's on fire

          first my lips get dry
                    so i lick them
& pretty soon my legs
              get tired &
everybody is drinking air
then the sun   a shrill lizard
& then   my chest cant   breathe it   hardly
its thirsty when they drink your wind

                    only my arms
in the back because where ive been
      holding them up
the heat goes heavy gone
hard Hawkeye keeps towing my shoulder
c'mon hawkeye cmon hawk you cn doit
& Tommy *gogogo* is yelling
this breath hawkeyes is trying

to catch me crunch crunch
crunch his cleats on the
cinders chewing like celery
breathing & sun & then
in a dizzy world im
& the sun goes
   off like a gun

        II

but then they come & get me
     after i fall down
the ears of leaves listening
& they give me a scar on the back
on my left foot look ill show you
to take home with me after my mom
took the bandage away & so i could run
again only i wasnt ever so fast
again when they let the fast out
through the crack in my foot

it made my foot so it
would want to skip its turn

        III

this is when i went to work with my dad
shovelling air with the bellows
so they would smile at you
the reds & yellows   in heat
i whistle   soft at them
hot with their eager
& at night the accordion shoves sounds
whittles them out like pancakes &

shoves them & the dancing
across the floor of my head
rocking my dad taught me when you
fall back on your hands & heels
dont kink your neck
& sneaking drinks   their sweat
& the beer & clapping
dippers full the air wet on the tin
& linda leaning over making
lanes in the lantern light
the windows when you go
outside to neck hang
like wet diapers

when my dead heel hurts too bad
& the dizzy blew thru me
blows me away like wind
i fall on the floor &
everyone laughs
like a balloon
laughed when the sun
ran & ran in my head

        IV

    but now   a lizard
    listens   a thin
    thread of light
    in the   nest
      of sun

s/he reads the weather

        in fall clouds
                shrug and bunch up
          old and grey and
          hang around in hunches
    a few squat on the porch
you can hear their stomachs growling

    nothing much happens
they scroll by in newsreels, the clouds
                smudgy and uncertain
                  which way to turn
                  and when they do
they slump into their shoulders and
              shove off

that s right s/he says and if i didnt believe it
i could see for myself come fall
    just wait ill see
says with a foolish grin
                & that's not just for show
                you know
think im just making this all up
    s/he says
        the doors fall open
    just watch
                they'll flop in the air like dog ears
    never fail
        and what's more they'll
make small sounds of footsteps when they go

bars of bright butter

the grasshoppers dry
    ticking there
under the boards
bars of bright butter
my skin stuck wet to leathers smooth & he
hell no no kinda pussy round here mister
so you can hear the oily
sssshlluuuullp when i move
& liphair darkbrown barrooming
killed my beard
the scissors his wrist
snipsnipsnipsnap
                  slowly
off the green tiles
dognails click on

          pans of sunlight
                    skirling
      every
    where
         every
way

spuds & gravy

sd slick warden Davey
to the tick of his shoe
*you big hunkie stud
got a treat for you*

& they spun me round
spuds & gravy
stung me with beans
that were navy

sung me with beans
so unsavoury
they slung me round
spuds & gravy

lord sez judge Gordon
*get a kick out of this
you slip this cord on
& yr bound for such bliss*

spun me & stung me
sung me & slung me
swung me round
spuds & gravy

yes sung me & stung me
slung me & swung me
they strung me round
new spuds & gravy

look

    there
        under the steps
    you can feel the cool
           & the moist against
                yr cheekbones
        the fine hairs on yr arms
            slats of light
          nailed on a picket fence to
    the black below

smell of must
           & the cat
      an orange bale of sunlight
          sskk skk skk
      cmere Scraggles
          thru the damp
        the long whiskers
    across the lathes
          2 green parentheses shine
  at you
      cmon cmon tom

     & then the crying
        a rabbits
      high squeal like
          a terrified baby
                  crying
        a rabbit dangles from
  a cats mouth
      screaming
    & screaming

like hens flopping

       the sun
      you can
      smell it
in the cracks
  of shingles
         it is
       pulling
    the nails
rraaaawwk
        rrawk
hens in dust
                flopping

pennys from heaven

                    : in
coming
                bundles of light :
   out of the blue
                    thudding
            on to her cornea scratching
                me in
       side the wet optic rope
                    where wafers of sun scuttle
            along like electric coal cars
                whistling
    in to the bumps dumping
                    their sticks of TNT in to
                        crevices in to

                    the nervous gaps/
                                burnt
inside her brain

                bends
                        out thru the
        two bubbles
        raining blue/
                    light
                            trans
        lucent
                    as cuticles
        curves out onto
                    in gusts
                            up
                        on
                me

                we too
                we two to
    gether
)gather
                ing
        light

she thinks of him

        absent minded
        find traces   of you

till out of the jelly they will
   come   the heat of eyes
   surprise me   they are blond
   blind with regret

      the ache of blood   in the head
         my whole body   remembering you

expecting / the sun

                                  it has
                   jumped down
         upon her
the sun
          has jumped
                 & soon now
                         the moon
            strolls slow
                     beside her
  low inside her
            like a white
                   foot

                   (floating)

at the montcalm

stones of light/
                    lo Penny
            sliding
                      inside yr hand
    as if tins of linseed oil
              sidling
sd *good to see you John.*
Penny.
          Penny sad
                bin thinkin ya

        Penny beside in beersmoke & chips
                      beer falling
            like cotter pins
                  cool into the bins
        of yr mind
                folding you there

like a stone burns you when it's hot
        sparrow molecules peeping
    into you your
warm marrow blood
your copper brain idling
editing

          so——oo
                  whadya bin doin yrself
                      these days eh

narrow cylinders of beer
        harrows over shale rattling
    off sparks
            orange spangles off
  her tits her nipples

                            & bam a lawnsprinklering of tiny
sunspots fired
                John on brain
         four ball bearings roll over all over
               the floor thru clunkclunkclunk pinball culverts John
                                    on fire
John
    ha—ay John
I'm talking you
             pigging the O_2
                  heart to carburetor heats up
                        mixing up
      the fat in ravines runs off below
starting the meltdown
                starting
                        whats the matter
               with you Penny staring
     to uncore
    running smooth
      on high octane pining now

    into neck shoulders hands
how i luv ya how i
         luv ya
          so you get up a good head of steam
                waiting for
           just when
       you cn shove er
             Jesus Jack
       to the floor
           & rip right thru
      the brownpaper bag
        just like a runway
     kidney

i wanna talk to you

hay no no wait
wait a minute willya
c'mon wai'minute
c'mon back here eh

aaww come on
i wannt talk to you

i take it back
all those things
i said
don go away

haaaayyy

sshhhii—lITTT

my god what'll Audobahn say
sons a bitches words
clitterin off like
sparrows gorged on rotten grain
really packed it in there

juhEEEsus jumpin christ
look at the bare assed little buggers go
hoppin like red peppers
can you beat that

                        aaw hell
                        there's no way of
                        getting them back
                        is there

  no i dint think so
whole goddamn world's gonna be
overrun by ripped birds
full of those flaming assholes
        spoiled rotten
squeaking & peeping
& squirting shit all over the place
                & sweet fuck all
                you can do about it
                is there
                eh

may day

                                        sulphur
                    weeds
                            whhoo   *oooshh*
   sun scratches
        them on

                           then
      puffs of
          clouds tubercular
                           gathering
     a saltwater sky

                 at dusk still sun
           sifting under eyes shifting red dust &
                                          sudden
                      bullets of rain

                              Portage & Main

            trampolining
off the steps

skipping rope

        1 2 3
           a larry
three little kids
    on Wellington & Academy
       skipping
  girls on both ends
        paisley & pinafores
    the rope slopping
        round in their sticky hands
like a shaving brush
      & the sun rains thru
          cotton lifting off the poplars
        in parachutes

the boy jumping high
in the air like a
frightened frog
   his feet
in dirty runners flapping

        4 5 6
           a larry
       7 8 9
           a larry

rope slapping the sidewalk
      & the blondes
    in giggles
hands over their mouths

        7 8 9
          a larry
          10 a larrrrr eeee
     ca—aaatch
            meeee

       yanking

          the rope tight
           & the kid

thrown into the dirt

his knees skinned
a young kid with black hair
spits dirt & screams
     bitchesbitchesbitches

   girls in giggles running
   running to St. Mary's

in a dark room

Westlake
      down the hall
           the step & the
    stops the camera stepping
              up the hall

        smell him
          crouched
            it's him
          there at the table
              small on the other side
      where yellow shims
                the bottom of the door
      odour of tap water running

    you know
              the Free Press ink he's reading
            his breathing in
    under the tiniest crackings
of tin in his wrists
        the lunging
            of air on teeth & spittle

          where he behind the door &
      going home soon
    his tobacco pouch
opened   )look you will see
      when in the day they shave open
                  the doorlock.

  brown of it smells
thru 40 feet of my dark here
      blocking me
           behind

       rows and rows of overnight trunks
          parked right to the ceiling

)hear his hair shoving thru skin
               & airdust
   on the new whiskers in his lip
whispers
      sleeping now in
             & out
    under

                 the one light
         dropped / over him
           a braid of current
        slung inside the
    pinch of old piss & cooked turnips
     the damp-paper torch of air
on this side of day

    warehoused on this side
         1 week's sweat
     in unchanged shorts
  fastened
        onto the blanket itch
    the fibres of
       night they wrap
you in

      but one bulbfist is shedding its
    fatness losing
  its fight with
    the yarn of smoke
       on his eyeglasses
   & the white fork

      hauling black out
                            side that window
            the lift tractoring under
eggcrates of night

           wheeling them out
               5 big tines
        for the first time

jump out at you
     in at you
             a white paper sky
                         coming
                    coming at you
                            fastfastfastfastfastfastfastfast

once in a blue moon

drinks
in the kitchen   laughing
bunch of the guys   few guests
winging it
Benny being skinny
in his shorts begins skiing sky
high on beer & gin
the spirits snake in him
squeeze thru the esophagus
bobsled the moguls *whumpwhump*
in his stomach like ghosts
they wind down the course   coast
into the foot of the slope
grin crayoned all over his face

bit queasy at first
                    trembles
Benny by a chair bent
in a neat tuck then
a wicked flash of light
Harv thumbs a match behind him and
Benny *wwhhuuuupp* Benny
becomes a profane torch
blasting the cold behind him
getting wind of a good thing
he becomes it / it becomes him
a grand mariner setting sail
Benny benign as a bishop on grand marnier
going out in a blaze of glory
you remember Bell   the silly fart
singed all the hair off
his ass when he mooned on us
he asked for it

we aghast what a gas
step back shaken when
Benny   who wld have
guessed he had a ghost of a chance either
Benny a flaming asshole all right
in a burst of blue phosphors night

Benny lit   Benny alight
his soul on fire
his eyes blue with ecstasy
he is pulling in to heaven blind
he who has seen / has become / the wind
whosoever has passed the wind
he is in an other world
beyond jesting now he is just
dead to the world

Benny burns in a pure blue ether
whyn the soule dypartes

Sonya Orlowsky

They say in Plum Coolee there's this old Ukrainian lady she can cure cancer. You know the Mennonites how they are always comin down with some kind of sickness or other. One time it's pneumonia, nother time it's they're simple in the head. Not one thing it's another. That's why they keep lookin for other men, the women there. Somethin about needin new blood on account of they're always marrying each other that causes all kinds of troubles for them—so babies dead when they're born or they've got one leg shorter than the other maybe or they've or they've got their eyes crossed, that sort of thing. Sure, some people say they go just crazy at times the women there sometimes they're kind of mixed up crabby with women's troubles I guess and wantin dark men somethin bad but I dunno, can't say about that one.

Anyways, this lady, Sonya Orlowsky's her name, she's Ukrainian and she can cure cancer, that's what they say at least. You might know her, remember she was just, well, one good-lookin woman at one time, apparently, they say, back round the 80's the one you musta heard it when Garry Reed left his wife and six kids and ran off with that dark woman well that was her, caused a real stink with his folks, never talked to him after, not once in all those years since then. Funny, n she the best liked schoolteacher district ever had too. Still got a way with men, I mean that's the story you get at any rate, isn't it?

But that's not what I was gonna tell ya. She has this, I dunno, this whatchemecallem, a kind of power I guess you'd say. Ever since she was 13, 14, and startin to turn a few heads in town she's had it. It's kind of strange I mean a guy doesn't know what to make of it eh but, well, they say she just puts her hand on the growth, real gentle, always the left hand for some reason I hear. Say it's on the neck here and she'll just hold it there for awhile, maybe 2, 3, minutes say and then, when she lifts it, the growth's gone. It's in her hand there, small white octopus they say. But the crazy thing is there's not sposed to be any scar left over. It's gone, every last sign of it's completely gone. Hands like that. I know that's hard to believe but I've talked to dozens of people from out that way and they all say that's what happens, they swear to God it's true, every last one of them swears she just lifts the hand and there it is the cancer's gone, just like that. Layin right there in her hand.

Think that's amazin, wanna hear something really strange? All the people, all the ones had those growths removed, know what they do after? They go and pickle them. That's right, they put them up in jars and set them in their sitting room where everyone can see them. Callin by Karl Dyck's and his missus the other day, day it rained, week ago Tuesday must a bin, to pick up some eggs and there she was—a big white blob in this sealer, right there plop on top of the radio. Karl was pretty pleased about it, took down the jar and give it to me so's I could get a good look at it floatin round like a pig's foot in vinegar. Don know what he was thinkin but did he get a kick out of it, but to tell the truth it give me the willies. Got no stomach for them things but I guess it don bother the Dycks one little bit, they just passed it round like was one of those big French parsnips if you ever seen one of them, seemed to think it was something special we were all sposed to drop our drawers at or somethin. Funny thing's even the little girl, what's her name, the little one always giggles, yeah—Caroline, Caroline—she watched it like she was a cat fishin, know how they just sit there and stare and stare.

i see them sawing

rumble of stacking

the sweet smell
new lumber in the sun
its smells let out
when the sawing is done to them
& the once in awhile high sound
where the wood fights back
there is the sap running
out where they give the cuts
the men bending
over in a strange geometry of need
the veins sliced open stream with resin
sharp odour in the afternoon sun
the shadow strangely slows
when the pain drains out of the wood

    roots   branches   leaves

they finish it off with nails
a dead frame they nail together
they put me on to
morrow a dying body on a drying rack
billions of cells held
by their sentence

the men in their long robes
who sit up there
putting me on
it

---

notice how the author avoids drawing out the possibilities of the menstruating tree and the dryness of the gallows—a clear sign of male power overtaking the matriarchal.

It must have been tempting: to insist on this connection or at least to try it out under the pressure of certain positions.

my deerest Jion,
    they said you have lost
the court appeal and know, there is no more chance
for you at all my love they say weel be
a lone the kids and me, i red about it
in the papers garie you remember him tost
on the portsh this morning and i could onely glance
at what they sad i just cant see
what they ment when they sed it fit
the crime. that may be right for them Jion
but its coled in bed at night and Dans
bin asking for you to and once I dremt
how you wuld tutsch me close and we wuld roll on
the bed was warm and all over your hands
and your eyes your eyes my love but i was emti
when i woke up it was so cold + Im showting your name
and i shall never forget you my love.
                as always
                your jipsy lady
                    Janicia
your dad is feeling   xoxoxo
    kind of
    bad

high drama

Music. "Penny's Song." Builds. They touch but draw back, suddenly.
KRAFCHENKO (*silence*) What's wrong?
PENNY (*silence*) I don't know. I just don't feel right about it, somehow. Not where everybody's looking. (*She looks anxiously out at the readers. She avoids K's eyes.*)
Ha—ay not now, they can see everything, John. And I'm not one of those girls will take her clothes off for "art." (*While they are talking a light comes on suddenly, revealing* cooley, *up stage, in a cone of light. He is carrying a script in his hand.*)
COOLEY (*to you, dear reader*) Why don't they make love? (*to them*) Hay! What are you doing? (*they look up, discovered*) I want you to make love. I'm pretty disappointed in you characters, especially you Krafchenko. (*Sheepish, they try to cover up. Penny adjusts her hair. Kraf, after the first split second of uncertainty, starts to rise.*) Give you a chance like this & what happens?
KRAFCHENKO (*recovered*) Butt out buddy. It's none of your business. (*Kraf & Penny begin to kiss. Defiant, then lost in it. Cooley looks angry & impatient.*)
COOLEY NO, no! Can't you get it right? It says here, look, it says: "But they soon feel awkward & pull away. Penny sighs." See, the stage directions immobilize you. The stage directions do not allow you to fool around. Now. Not now they don't. Not once I get here. It's too late then, you blew your chance. (*They start to grope & nuzzle. Not listening.*) Not now I said. (*murmurs of protest*) No, I mean it. Now. According to the script, Kraf, you get yr ass outa here. Then Penny is supposed to make a play for me. I wrote it that way. A clear case of textual authority. Of my authority. My authorization. So, way you go now, Kraf. I'll look after things from here on in.

(KRAF *goes, looking back, doubtful. She turns to* cooley, *upset, her eyes large with dark. A crow calls, offstage.*)

this is me: a retort

a pale spectacle to you
my hands my eyes
my body who was here

drawn from me
to you dead
apparently
my mercury vapour still
alive it moves
under the sun reading
light & shadow
shaking radiance out of
silver grains

ancient planets hurtle
through dark rooms shudder out
strange-smelling chemicals
dipped in those pans
sun pens brightness
another version
on your jelly eyes

if you look close
you can touch the
envelope of light
by my light
you can read
inklings of me

somewhere beneath winnipeg
my face is flushed
away in quick lime
    & yet
this is a glimpse of me

burnt out the rays
reaching you
only now this glow is me
your vision of me
my body gone
utterly silent

a silver figure
your Venus eyes
shining

ruderal

        me a lime flower
gorged on garbage
                now i am
pressed to death
      between their words

            by the weight of their words im
    pressed flat in that diction
           airy i float
        my body pulped
                     to slime in a sink
            draining the bouquet
                  all the juicy parts away
                          my breath
          fading beneath their cowls
              their scowl of eyes

            seized in their eyes
yeseyeseyeseyeseyeseyeseyeseyeseyeseyeseyeseyeseyeseyeseyeseyeseyeseyeseyeseyeseyeseyeseyeseyeseyeseyese

                   canonized

           me a lime flower gorged on their
              refuse

night vision

                                the milky way /
                                    sways on sky
                         brilliant daubs
                                they say stars are
                        a choker of sperm
swung from her neck

other side   :
                                a finger of light
                       grips the air
                           :   Fitzgerald
                       carrying fire in his hand
           makes his rounds
                       his halo of tobacco
he dangles a nail of light
               into my dark
           you ok kraf
                       sticks it into my eyes
                    yeah shit im fine eddie

                       fire carrying my dead away
                       like a hot fender
                                just fine

mooning

          moon wandering
                  all over   the place
    & me wondering what
       its like
nothing ive done before
          will i like
 to be man
in the moon to be soon
manning the moon
man to be high on air
looks fair to me

to be that moon
moonin for me
& me for she
to be a sigh
in there oh to be
putting on airs
such heavenly affairs
spooning the moon
moon spooning musk
melon over me

you are there

                    yes i see you
there
    on yr side of the page
        past brooms of night
the cigarette there/
                beside you
      its ashes crashed like a broken pencil
    the cat warm in the lamp

    it is late &
Mozart clean so clean

    it is late but
you are listening to me

              i can hear
you shift in yr chair
reach across for the coffee
on the oak chest there beside you
you make a few notes in the margins
there is a flaw in
the paper you cld see
if you looked

        i can see you
    are annoyed
yes i can see that
            that i wld
    talk to you
        like this
      that my eyes (evangelist at yr
        door(look in at you
            wld look at you

you wish i wld
        go away
you wish you cld
        go to
bed yes make luv to
the young woman in green
    cords & dream
under crisp blankets
of rooms full of baptist virgins
rinsed in toothpaste
yr blue words like potato
chips floating into the auditorium
& 16 yr olds stepping
out of the showers
in mouthwash & shampoo

it is years & years
later & you
     seeing me here
             crouched on the paper breathing
     you behind the ink
   other side of this page
      hfhfhf   hfhfhf
                  you do not like
     that this my face wld
   come to you wild like this
like this yes you
          do
     unload on you smell of beer & garlic
    my hand tilts this way its fine
    dark hairs

            it is christmas & the lights
         drip into the room
in tiny electric colour
            like ribbon candy
                 later on we'll conspire

            reach thru
             to
ward you touching
        you touching me
      the bruise on my neck
            in yr head
        like a tire iron
                as we dream by the fire

                 my body
     38 presses & swelling
            of sweat inside the pine
                  of yr living
       room of
         the black hair
thick in yr face
      on yr neck
     spreading warm
        down yr body to
            these hands over you
                  & in
       you my breath
my hot hot breath
               in side of
      you

the obligatorylongawaited poem in which the hero speaks from the grave thots thick with gumbo

       yes yes well i spose cooley
       was a grave robber all along
       wasnt he

                this comes from
                knowing Foucault
                I told him so myself

& I spose I wulnt even get a peep in here if cooley wasnt interested in some
kind of parody. at least thats what he said when he tried to explain why im
here now why he was botherin me after all this time sd somethin bout
where wed end up & how hed prefer to keep middling along. doesnt know
where or when to call it quits.

but you want me to say something else dont you you want some
consolation some message from the other side well piss off none a that
crypto-fascism here you attend to the chores a living man can hope for a
cow right now thats what i come to tell you thats it thats all there is there is
no more its the cows when yr dead yr dead a mans a long time in the grave
get this thru yr thick skull a woman too

      i got no summary i got nothing to say theres nothing
a say
      except maybe Laws
that son of a bitch i make no bones telling you this
that son of a bitch is still callin the shots well look
around you sure hes cleaned up his act a bit picked up
a slightly prissy accent but check it out youll see
for yrself hes still there upholdin standards suckin
up to the imitation brits & the strongarm yanks see for yrself ya
dont believe me boring & bullying

        & penny i really miss her
cld you tell penny
i miss her bad
when you see her
im all skin & bones right

thinkin of her
nothin but a pile of bones now
you remember that to penny

that oughta get a rise outa her

miss penny

song after

oohh he was a handsome devil
in the dim view of limplimbed Bevel
you know how the ladies all treated him
& how he was so sweet on every quim

by the red

if you cant call now
call when you can
warm in your voice love
glad in your hands

you at my window
you at my door
hold me once more dear
hold me once more

leave you a letter
leave you this song
leave you my love dear
sayin so long

send me some words though
though they are numb
words to remember
when they will come

willows of green leaves
sprinklers of sun
spindles of air love
whiskey of sun

crow in a door dear
crow in a door
hungry for somethin
wont see you no more

so pay me a visit
pay me no heed
sun starts to rise
sun starts to bleed

headingly jail love
headingly jail
think of me penny
in headingly jail

by the red river
river so low
walk by the willows
blowing in snow

closing time

O.K., that's about it. Closing time folks. Drink up.
empties rattling. Can you drink up there. Closing,
sorry.
C'mon, drink up please. Nope, that's it. cloth
slurping up the wet.
Can ya just leave the glasses behind, you don't mind?
Night. See ya. Yyyyyuupp.

plenty of time for a
hang over tomorrow
tomorrow you will have one bitch
of hang over but tonight
tonight they are closing up

appendix

At the end of the system, at the juncture of the small intestine and the colon, is found a small pouch, called the cecum: a long, narrow worm, it burrows into the digestive tract at this point. An itch in the gut. Perhaps feeding like a tapeworm. Perhaps commensally, perhaps not. No one knows for sure what it does. Although the attachment ranges from as little as one inch to as much as nine inches, commonly it is three inches in length. I can't tell from the picture what colour it is, I can't even see it. It's not in the picture. Neither Gray nor Nilsson show it. But I know the worm is easily inflamed and, in acute cases, can be extremely dangerous. On occasion it has been known to burst open and to spew poison throughout the body.

A vestigial organ, apparently now useless, it tends to undergo obliteration as a functionless organ. It is commonly removed surgically to ensure the health of the body. This practice was common for children not so long ago. Oddly enough, not for Cooley. His appendix is intact.
[Editor's note: Once was intact, for it is no more.]

Well, I for one don't think there should have been an appendix.
It's silly.

Silly? It is an affectation if you ask me. It sticks out like a sore thumb. Headings and footnotes are permissible within reason. But an appendix. That's going too far.

Perhaps, dear reader, you would like to remove this appendix. Go ahead, just cut it out. You always wanted to be a doctor, here's your chance. Be careful to cut neatly so the body will not be mutilated and the scar will not be conspicuous enough to affect the resale value of the book or to ruin your practice. Perhaps, if you are lucky, you will nick Cooley's conscience, his mind there on the margins, in the gutter. Go ahead, take it out on him.

that's it

That's it. Give me that.

What?

The manuscript. I'm taking it now.

Now? I'm not done.

No, that's it Cooley, time's up.
It's getting too big and I'm taking it.

please refrain

                                          well this is so

                    unfinished &

                        so un

              polished

you can say that again

                          & so am i i m

              un im

                              pressed this is

              so am

                        ateur ish

        this is

                it

                                    you said it

              this is the living

          the living

                  and man

                      this is the living and

you mean that's it

                  and I

                      am on to

        you the living

            there can be no leaving

                                  believing

                              all this

                              ah this

        is really living

loving it

                what did I tell you

     this is

          is this

   it

                  is this

            all

          there is

                                all of oral or
                                                                all of
                        it
                      this
                   how un
                      be
            coming
that it should come to this
                                            particular and
                         and then
what more can i say
I've had it with this
what more do you want
            that's it then
                                no more
                                                            fraid not
                                                            fraid so
                                                            that 's it
                        nonsense
                                        what are we to conclude
       here
            right here
                the but
            ends of life

            what more can i say

                    what can i tell you
what do you want from me

at the bridge, penny—

    under the damp swallows

under the damp swallows slips a glittering yellow.
soon the glittering yellow thought of beside the bending assiniboine.
the bending assiniboine then never flipped within the yellow.

    away the yellow penny

away the yellow penny slides a shining sun.
slow the shining sun mauve along the thin water.
the thin water then near dipping within the sun.

    along the yellow bridge

along the yellow bridge washed a shining wind.
dimly the shining wind bending within the pale willows.
the pale willows then noisily tarred far the wind.

    above the damp assiniboine

above the damp assiniboine will hear a glittering bridge.
then the glittering bridge slips under the mauve swallows.
the mauve swallows then soon thought of beside the bridge.

    the yellow wind

the yellow wind then quick flip beside the willows.
the shadowed water then dimly slides away the wind.
far the thin penny slides a shadowed wind.

off the yellow sun

off the yellow sun dipping a shadowed water.
near the shadowed water tarred far the pale penny.
the pale penny then now slides within the water.